WORKPLACE ACTIONS MATTER

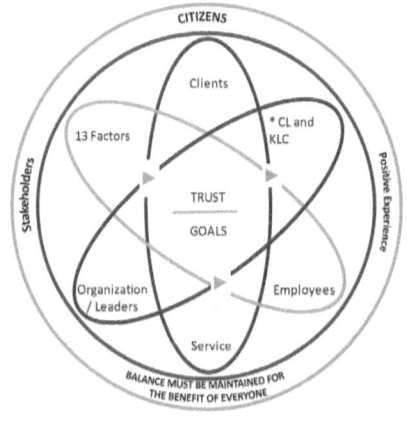

NATHALIE WHITE

Order this book online at www.trafford.com
or email orders@trafford.com

Most Trafford titles are also available at major online book retailers.

Print information available on the last page.

ISBN: 978-1-6987-1327-4 (sc)
ISBN: 978-1-6987-1325-0 (hc)
ISBN: 978-1-6987-1326-7 (e)

Library of Congress Control Number: 2022919985

Trafford rev. 02/24/2023

Trafford
PUBLISHING®   www.trafford.com
North America & international
toll-free: 844-688-6899 (USA & Canada)
fax: 812 355 4082

A big thank you…

To my husband for your unconditional love and
courage to continue this adventure with me.

To those who took the time to read my drafts
for your honesty and generosity of time.

To all my teachers throughout the years for your valuable counsel.

To you the readers for your support as we walk
through this amazing learning journey together.

Contents

Organizational Perspective

Bringing It All Together

Why Am I Writing This Book?

WHY NOT?

Unfortunately, I hear, too many times, complaints about the public service that I will not repeat here. I wanted to put out in the collective another perspective.

I wanted to show that you can learn and grow and have a wonderful life in the public service. Enclosed herewith are my learnings; my experience in the service to Canadians helped me grow and influenced my life and the one of my family. I would dare to say that it did save my life.

Why Should You Keep on Reading?

AGAIN, WHY NOT?

After thirty years in various roles in the public service, I started to think about what I wanted to do when I grow up. What is my next adventure? My reflection led me to think about all the people that influenced my leadership style over the years.

When I first started this leadership journey, there were no road maps available to me. I trusted my intuition as I navigated through different management roles. My background in employment counselling gave me a solid foundation to deal with people and teams. But that was it. I had interesting experiences along the way. I had to research my way out of my messes or challenges. This book contributes to the workplace by sharing my thoughts so that someone else can learn from my experiences.

I really have had a great career in the public service. It is where I could lead and influence others in a positive way. I feel fortunate to be able to say that my value as an individual was linked to my work. For me, work matters. This is where I found competence and acceptance of who I was as an individual and a professional. A big thank you to all of you for being part of this journey.

The next pages will give you the framework that has been evolving in my mind, which integrates all my learnings. I did not invent anything; I took some of the thoughts of great leaders and adapted them to my reality and applied them to the public service. Please note that I am still a learner. The words of this paper reflect my learnings today, and I am evolving. There are parts of this book that I will reflect where I am with the caveat that "there is more to come."

Was I successful? It depends on your definition of success. If I achieved all my objectives, then yes. If it is that my teams have received several awards through the years, yes. If it is that I reached a respectful level in the organization, again, yes. If your definition of success is the amount of people that were positively influenced by my leadership—they told me so—so yes! Finally, I can say that I am happy 92 percent of the time (this is a success in itself!), and this has lots to do with my work. Let me share with you what I learned.

First, you can read this book in any way your intuition tells you, sequentially as a whole or start at the chapter that inspires you. I suggest reading the foundation chapter, then have fun! The objective of this book is to provide you with foundational pieces of a business model that will frame your perspective for any role you choose. You will be able to go deeper in your learnings as your reality changes. It does not matter if you work in the public or private sectors. The approaches proposed here can be applied in both worlds.

In my experience, we are all leaders. Just by being human, we exercise leadership over the roles we play. "It is our contact and experience with other people that give your life joy, meaning and purpose" (Byrne 2021, 4). The minute our actions impact someone else, we need to be conscious of the consequences of our behaviors. Like it or not, we are making a difference in each other's lives.

You will read several times that work matters—it is a part of my brand. Why is that? For me, work provides the opportunity to follow the flow of life and live with authenticity. It provides the experiences to propel us into the future so that we can be the best version of ourselves and find joy. Nelson-Isaacs (2019) goes even further, insisting that once in the flow, we are not working anymore; we are playing (p. 173). As such, workplace actions matter. We need to remain conscious and listen to the messages that work brings to us. This is easier said than done! Let's look at some messages; Has any of these happened to you?

> - Not reached your organizational goals
> - Employees complaining or not engaged
> - Leaders managing status quo
> - Client complaints

> ➤ Failed an interview
> ➤ Hit a homerun

If you answered yes to any of these questions, please keep reading. You will receive information to view any organization holistically. This little book can even help you with the interview process for any leadership position.

THE FOUNDATIONS

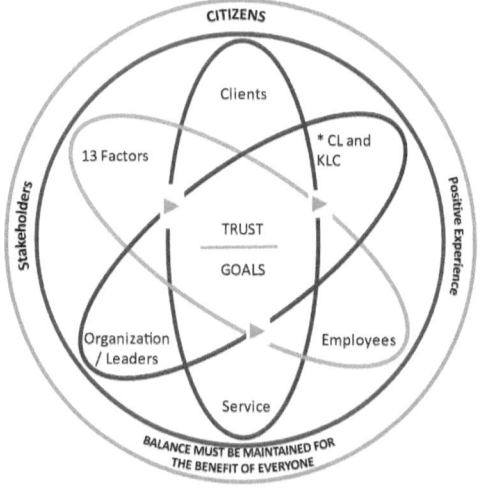

It Needs to Start Somewhere

THIS STORY IS NO DIFFERENT.

My journey started when one employee did not understand the definition of a "client." I was leading a process redesign workshop, and as much as I explained who the internal and external clients were, the employee still did not get it. I did some research to see how I could explain it differently. This is where I came across a little French book: *Qualité totale* (Kélada 2000). It changed my view of business and the public service.

In summary, actions are energy in motion.

The Atom graphic is the essence of my learnings and the impact of Kélada's teachings, which I adapted to the public service. The three critical dimensions of this model are the foundation for this book: clients, employees, and the organization (leadership).

I chose the atom to represent this relationship because of its power. The atom is the smallest unit of matter. It is made with everything in the universe; it has the power of being the source of nuclear energy. Likewise, at work, actions (toward clients, employees, or the organization) speak louder than words, and they have the power to either reinforce trust or hinder it. Atoms are the building blocks for chemistry, and at work, actions are the foundation of relationships. In sum,

Atom = Energy, Actions = Energy

It is at the junction of each (▶) that actions influence perceptions, expectations, confidence, and trust.

For example:

Junction of Organization/Employees: In my leadership role, if I tell employees that I have an open-door policy; but every time someone wants to come and see me, my door is always closed, and I am not available to meet with the employee because I am super busy. What is that telling the employees? This could potentially influence the expectations and trust that employees have in me because of my accessibility. There is a difference between what I say and do.

Junction Employees and Clients: This is when a client calls for a question on his file, but the employee is having a hard day, and he/she hurries the client to speak his mind. Even on the phone, the employee's demeanor can be felt by a client. You will see that a bad (or an OK service) does influence the client's perceptions in other activities, such as a government ability to govern.

The junction of Organization/Leaders and Clients can be felt several ways. Some can be direct, in the sense that if a client has a complaint and wants to talk directly to a supervisor, but it can also be indirect. The way a leader will support his/her employees will affect the work and services to clients. You will later see that if an employee brings their best version of themselves at work, it will influence the quality of the service, which, in turn, influence the perception of clients.

Likewise, if an employee does not deliver consistently, a leader might not have confidence that the employee can perform other tasks related to its work. It might take longer to collaborate and provide answers because of this lack of trust.

As you can see in the examples above, the smallest actions can make a big difference.

Furthermore, if one of the dimensions is absent, the enterprise does not exist (Kélada 2000). Just try it. Try to imagine a world where there are no clients. No employees or even no owners. It is impossible. In this model, you need to attend to the three dimensions to have a balance for a quality service or product. Kélada provides the example of the colors in a television (Kélada 2000, 39). If one of the colors (red, blue, or green) are out of balance, you will not have a quality image.

In my role as a public servant, at any given time, I am part of this trilogy. For example, when I gave birth to my child, I applied for benefits, and I became a client of that service. I was also a leader in the public service (organization) and received benefits as an employee. Depending on which hat I wear at any given time, it will influence my perspective and what I will pay attention to. This is especially real for me when my experience is not aligning with my expectations and my own individual goals.

How Does This Relate to Me?

YOUR GOALS MAKE A DIFFERENCE.

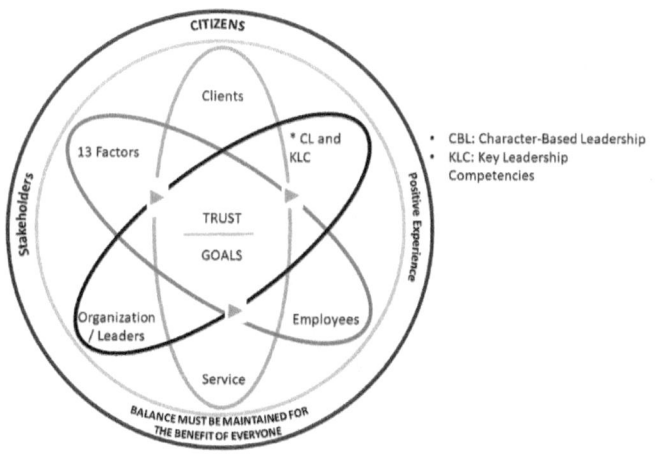

Now, let's go back to the graphic. The first thing you need to do is identify why you do what you do. Any organization, individual, or business has goals, such as a vision or mission. The goal in public service is to provide goods and services for the citizens. It is important that everyone can answer the following questions: What is it you are trying to achieve? What is your value? What is your goal or vision? I am using all these words interchangeably but fundamentally, What is the reason you get up in the morning?

Let's say, I want to go visit my friends, Lance and Del. I need to know that they live in Nelson, British Columbia. If I start driving from New Brunswick, and I do not know where they live, I might meet all kinds of great people along the way, but I might end up in Arizona because the weather is amazing, but I will have not visited Lance and Del.

Back to operations, it is important to be explicit of our goals as there are stakeholders, such as unions, lobby groups, etc., that will put pressure on this balance to fulfill their own agenda. This does not have to be complex; having an idea of what you want to accomplish will provide you with a sense of direction. In any operation, the balance of these three dimensions is both a science and an art.

This motivation (personal or professional) is essential. As such, if not realized, it will affect our satisfaction at work. We all work to achieve a goal, even if it is simply to make money! Or else, I know I would be on a permanent vacation! Any activities or behaviors will either bring us closer to our goals, or not. The impacts of our behaviors will either have positive or negative consequences on achieving these goals. As we saw, the junction of our interactions will affect the trust that each party has for each other.

The enclosed banner provides a summary of this section. It is at your advantage to answer these questions authentically. As an example, my motivation at work is to create healthy work environments. This is my passion. I get frustrated when my supervisor micromanages me and limits my actions or my creativity. I feel that he/she does not trust me, and I get impatient, which, in turn, affects the service I deliver to my clients and my employees.

Points of Reflection

1. First, identify what is it you want to achieve in your existing role.

2. What is important for your organization, clients, and employees?

3. Identify what are the activities and behaviors that create trust.

4. Can you identify the activities or behaviors that limit trust?

5. How do you know this to be true? What is your source of data?

6. How are you maintaining a balance that is consistent for the benefit of everyone involved?

What is The Big Deal?

TRUST IS HARD TO GET AND EASY TO LOSE.

This concept of trust is foundational for everything that we do. Stephen Covey's *The Speed of Trust* (2016) highlights three big ideas about making trust real in the workplace (see table below). In his own words, "This is the one thing that changes everything." It is what makes a difference in creating the successful relationships.

Trust Tax		
Economic Driver	Speed (low) Cost (high)	Speed (high) Cost (low)
Leadership Competency	Energy (low) Joy (low)	Energy (high) Joy (high)
Learnable Competency	Credibility (low) Character (to develop)	Credibility (high) Character (balanced)

Big Idea No. 1: Trust is an economic driver through a trust tax. When there is no trust, the speed of collaboration will take longer, and it will cost more time. I will ask more questions if I do not trust the information in front of me. The reverse is a *trust dividend*. When trust exists, the speed to accomplish a task will increase and the overall cost will go down (e.g., there will be no need to double-check the data in front of me).

Big Idea No. 2: Trust is the number one competency for leadership needed today. It makes the leadership job easier when there is trust. It transforms perspectives and learning occurs.

Trust Tax: When the trust goes down, the energy of the employees, and the joy to be at work goes down as well.

Trust Dividend: When trust is up, the employee's energy (engagement) is up, and the joy (job satisfaction) is also up. Try it; remember when you trusted that your supervisor had your back? How did that look and feel? Now, think of a time you did not trust that your supervisor had your back. How did it feel when you got home? How was your energy level?

Big Idea No. 3: Trust is a learnable competency. Trust is a skill practiced through our credibility and behaviors. Credibility is developed through character with a win-win intent and integrity.

In the chapter on the organizational perspective, I will go deeper into character dimensions. This idea is empowering; even if there is no trust, it is possible to create the conditions for success. Covey (2016) highlights the importance of extending trust to get trust. It just takes a little courage and humility to get the job done. Sometimes, our experiences with others require that we suspend our judgments, be present, and be open to other perspectives.

Recently, I started a new job. I had informal discussions with all the leaders. In one particular interaction, I did not get a good feeling. I stopped and listened to what was going on in my body. The feeling I got was that I needed to remain open. This person was seeing me for the first time, and I needed to gain his trust. Our behaviors make a significant difference in the quality of our relationships.

I have been playing with this concept, especially if my first impressions are not positive. I am purposely extending an invitation to change my mind. Sometimes, it goes well, other times, not so much. Just like in the above example, my first impression of this colleague was not positive, but there was no experience for me to base my perception. It was just a feeling. I listened to this feeling by proceeding with openness, but with a little caution.

It was deliberate actions repeated time and time again that created positive experiences in each of my roles in the organization. The consistency, competence, care, and commitment to consciously attend to my actions makes a difference (Russel 2012). Obviously, one needs to take the time to dedicate the energy for a conscious action, to be open to change and question our past assumptions about a situation.

I found that when I created trust in my relationships, I was honest and vulnerable. I found that with trust, there is no place to be politically correct or tell part of a story. Trust is unforgiving; it has its own radar. Therefore, I needed to be the complete version of myself, warts and all. I needed to be authentic with my boss, my employees, my clients, and myself.

In researching this topic, I found this article from Hannah L. Miller (2022) that brings it home for me: "10 Ways of Building Trust as a Leader" (leaders.com)

Consistently follow through on your commitments. Consistency makes a big difference in all aspects of life. If I cannot make it, I follow up and explain myself.

Quickly admit and amend mistakes when they're made. It takes courage, but it is worthwhile.

Communicate with emotional intelligence. Learning to interact and deal with people is a learnable skill. It requires me to slow down and pay attention to the queues in my environment.

Appropriately manage changes and pivots. I dedicated a few chapters to managing change. It does not have to be perfect to be successful, just an openness to learn.

Show appreciation and gratitude. Coming from a place of gratitude is where I show strength and support for my employees.

Eliminate judgment from work environments. This one is a hard one. I use a systematic approach to explore innovative ideas. I like to use facts and data to determine the impacts of a solution on the work and the clients. This approach helps me to stay curious and leads me to unpredictable solutions.

Don't dismiss the power of vulnerability. Again, still working on this one. Especially since I just started a new job, I have a hard time being in a learning mode. I feel, because of my experience and education, I should be competent right away. I relate to this advice as being human. Be present with my employees and relate to them on a human level.

Set clear expectations. That is a factor that supports a psychologically safe work environment.

Don't share information that isn't yours to share. Confidentiality is paramount to creating trust in the workplace. Listening and spreading rumours or misinformation do not add any value. For me, it goes back to Rumi's three gates: Is it true? Is it necessary to be told? Is it kind?

Be decisive and act with confidence and belief. This is a balancing act for me with being vulnerable. Especially since right now, I am starting a new mandate. I do have belief and confidence in my experience.

As I write these words, I am reminded that I will publish this book, and I will show the world my learnings. This makes me vulnerable as I am exposing myself, and at the same time, I am confident because these are my learnings. They created value for my employees, my clients, my organization, and me. It is my wish that it does the same for you. I truly believe in this, and I let it go.

I will leave you with an anagram for trust:

> **T**he employees are
> **R**elying on your
> **U**nderstanding
> **S**imply
> **T**reat them well

In summary, to create an environment of trust we need to be conscious, accept imperfection, learn, and grow with our employees, clients, or the organization.

In conclusion, the words of Dr. John Demartini (2021) provide a great summary for this chapter:

> I think that all business is actually teaching, and I teach this in my corporate training, all businesses are teaching people how to open their hearts, be authentic, and maintain sustainable fair exchange with shareholders, customers, employees, and society. It's actually the divine way of trying to teach people how to be their authentic soul.

In other words, work matters!

At the end of the day, we all want to achieve our goals. In order to succeed, we need a model to help navigate through the complexity of any organization. In my years in a leadership role, this framework has delivered in spades. Let's look at the details.

> *Thank you, Mr. Joseph Kelada and Mr. Steven Covey. Your bodies of work have influenced my mindset. I was able to implement this perspective in everything I do, which resulted in a successful career and positive results for citizens.*

"*Note to Self*"
Learning Solutions

_____

_____

_____

_____

_____

_____

_____

_____

_____

THE CLIENT PERSPECTIVE

Why Should We Care?

BECAUSE WE ALL HAVE BEEN THERE.

Have you ever experienced . . .

- a miserable service?
- an OK service?
- a really great service?

What was the difference? Is it the person? How many hoops had you had to jump through? Was it a question of timeliness of the service? Quality of the product? The flexibility with which you accessed the service? The cost of the overall experience? I would guess the answer is a little bit of everything.

What happens if you get great service? Most people would talk it over with friends and family. The essential thing, though, is that you will return to the same store to get that service. This is where brand recognition is powerful.

We will see that for the government, it goes a step further. It will influence the confidence that we have in the capacity of the government to represent our interests. This is powerful; the services we receive can influence the way we vote.

Spoiler alert! The enclosed banner contains nine activities that explain the full book. As you can see, there is hope; there is science to madness. Let's look at the details that influence our experiences when assessing a service or product.

IMPROVEMENT APPROACH

1. Look at an activity in your world that brings you pain.
2. Evaluate it from a perspective of cost, quality, and flexibility in doing business, and timeliness of service.
3. Map out the steps that reflect the sequence of activities.
4. Look at the value that each brings.
5. Ask why, why, why, why, why, why, do the steps need to exist.
6. Determine how they can either be eliminated or refocussed to add more value.
7. Measure the whole thing.
8. Review your results.
9. Do some testing.
10. Roll-out.
11. Document your experience.
12. Repeat the whole process.

What Does Processes Have to Do with It?

THE ACTIVITIES ARE ALL INTERRELATED.

To explore what is going on behind the scene, I will use an example of when I had to apply for benefits.

When I stopped working to have my baby, I had to apply for benefits. The first step was to fill out the form. I needed to validate my identity. The information was electronically sent for processing and validation. If everything was OK, then I became eligible to receive benefits. If more information was required, like proof of my baby's birth, then delays could occur, especially if I did not have the information handy.

If you ever applied for any type of benefit, you know that these steps can take a few minutes to hours or months to be processed. What was happening?

Dr. Michael Hammer's definition of a process has always been my guiding light to explain how work gets done:

> A process is a related
> group of activities that
> together creates a result
> of value for the clients.
> (Hammer 2002)

Each of the words means something. A *group* of activities is a series of steps to achieve an outcome. It takes all the steps that create the value, not just one. My identity needed to be validated so that I can prove I am who I say I am to be eligible for these benefits.

The activities are *related* and *organized*. They are designed in a certain way to get the results we want. It is a logical stream. It is not random or ad hoc; you need to input the information in the computer in order to receive the benefits. We see delays in a process when some of these activities are skipped or errors are made along the way.

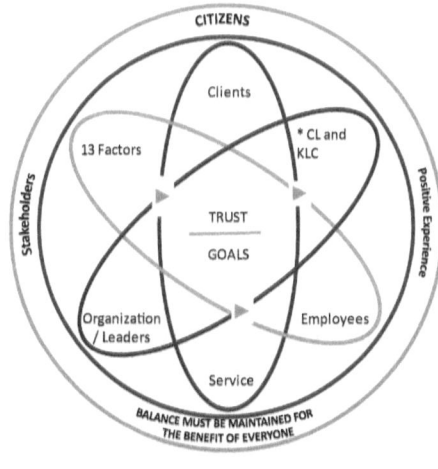

They are merging *together* toward a certain goal. In the above example, it is to provide accurate and timely benefits to a client. All employees involved in the steps (reception, agents, and call centers) need to work to achieve this result. For example, if I call to inquire about my benefits, the call center agent needs to ensure that my application is complete before hanging up the phone. If call center agents are measured by the amount of time spent on the phone, they will want to answer my questions quickly and move on to the next caller. When additional information is required to complete the processing, it could interfere with the overall client goal—*the results.*

These behaviors force us to look at the organization systematically to provide a *result of value* for the clients. These processes have a purpose; they are trying to achieve something. They do not exist just for the sake of existing. As we have seen in the previous chapter, each action taken by the employees (see arrows in graphic above) at all levels (call center, reception, processing, and leadership) can either create a positive or negative experience for the clients.

The use of a process map makes the process visible. I used so many process maps in my years that I used to have a nickname—Mapthalie—which I am proud of. If my colleagues retain one piece of information, it would be to map your process in order to improve it. Wow, how powerful!

Before I go further, there is a need to explain that there are different levels of process representations. One can talk to the system, macro processes, processes, and micro or subprocesses and procedures. One needs to understand where they fit into the big picture to understand the level that they are talking about.

When we look at improvements, it is better to work at the system, macro or process levels, to make significant improvements. Otherwise, there is a risk to improve something that should not be performed at all.

If we are aiming for incremental changes, then the micro (sub) process and procedure levels are appropriate.

Example of levels:

System	Macro	Process	Micro (Sub)	Procedures
Making a Living	Working	Getting to Work in the Morning	Getting Clean	Details to Take a Shower or Bath
Entertainment	Watching TV	Looking at a Hockey Game	Enjoying Food	Cooking Popcorn
Provide Value for Clients	Human Resource Management	Onboarding	Security Clearance	Fingerprints

In the example above, let's say we all have to make a living. I could be working very hard at improving my morning routine to go to work. I could wash the night before so I do not waste time in the morning; I might save seven minutes. This would be considered an incremental improvement compared to me winning a substantial amount of money where I do not have to go to work at all (substantial gain).

The same is true that, if for my entertainment, I choose to go skiing instead of watching TV, my planned activities would be different all together.

The use of maps is great for exploring ideas, such as brain maps, or even for training employees on a service. Let's take the example of having supper; after all, we all must eat. What are they key steps?

Before you look at my list, take a moment and make your own list.

"*Note to Self*"
Learning Solutions

_____

_____

_____

_____

_____

_____

_____

_____

_____

My results:

Feeding the Body

Before	During	After

| Need for nourishment | Feel like cooking? Y | Look for food | Found something? Y | Prep food | Cook | Do Table | Eat | Do dishes | Digest | Satiety |

N → Order out

N → Look again in Fridge

Food something? Y / N

Look again in Pantry

Found something? Y / N

I am sure that your list is different than mine. I will take again Dr. Hammer's key words in the process definition and see how it applies here:

Group of activities: In order to eat, I need to do something. Either I make supper or order out, but actions are going to be performed.

Related and organized: There is a logical sequence to the activities. I need to prepare the food first before serving. If I want to eat, all the activities need to be bringing me closer to this goal. If I start watching TV while cooking and forget my food on the stove, I will not be eating tonight.

Together: In order to eat, I will need to buy food, cook, and serve. I need to do all these activities in order to have something to eat.

Result of value: The fulfillment that I will get from the experience will depend on my initial goal: make spaghetti or a steak or order out? We will see that this result could also be influenced by the quality and quantity of the food. My experience could also be influenced by how much it cost me to eat this food. The impact on my bank account.

The purpose identified for this process is to nourish the body. I might want to do things differently if it was to nourish the body and the soul, or do I? The activities will differ depending on my objectives. They need to be consciously designed.

Does Each Activity Have a Meaning? You Ask

OF COURSE, THEY DO. WE JUST LEARNED THAT!

The lesson that I learned early in my career (and that served me well) from Dr. Michael Hammer referred to ETDWB (easy to do business with). It does not matter who the client is, whether it be internal, external, your employee, your boss, or your colleague. What is their experience? Is it easy to interact with you, your team, your organization? Basically, would you like to deal with *you*? If the answer is no, then it would be in your interest to change it.

The 2020 Citizens First study (July 8, 2021) shows that if a client contacts the government, they expect resolutions of their issues within eight minutes on the phone and six minutes online. After twenty minutes of interactions with the websites or a contact person, the satisfaction decreases significantly (up to twenty points for the phone).

Every action with the client's experience will influence their satisfaction and confidence in the government. It is that experience that will create trust, or not. The Institute for Citizen-Centred Service called these moments of truth. Therefore, it is imperative to understand the business processes associated with any service or the creation of any product.

Most of the time, we know we are not getting the results we want, but we do not know why. We might be unsure of the direction to take. Even if we have a process clearly identified, what does it mean? Are the steps appropriate? I used this little exercise to teach what was value-added, non-value-added or business value, and waste activities.

This time I will take the example of watching a hockey game comfortably at home. What do you expect when you see a hockey game? Some participants will say fights, playing hockey, socialization, commercials, penalties, cleaning the ice, etc.

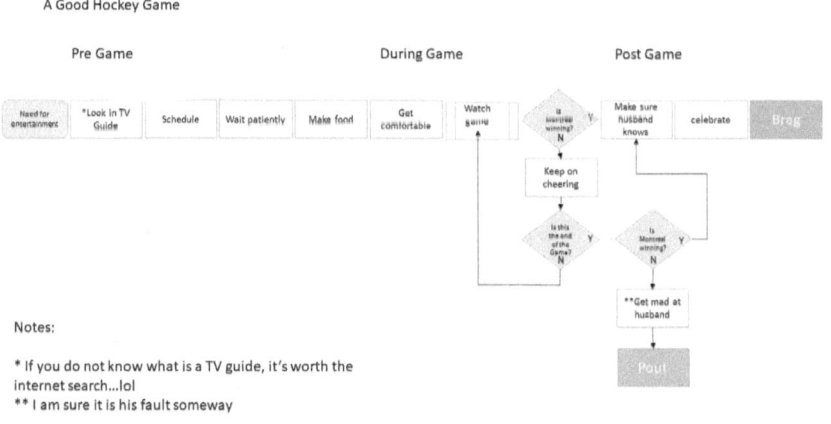

At the process level, the map could look something like the above. If you find yourself doing more pouting, you might question yourself to see if watching a hockey game is the right entertainment for you. Even if Montreal wins, my experience will be either positive or negative. It all depends on what happens when I am watching the game. The "watch game" steps are what we call value-added. I need and want that step to occur when I watch a hockey game (or else, what is the point?). Now, let's look at this subprocess.

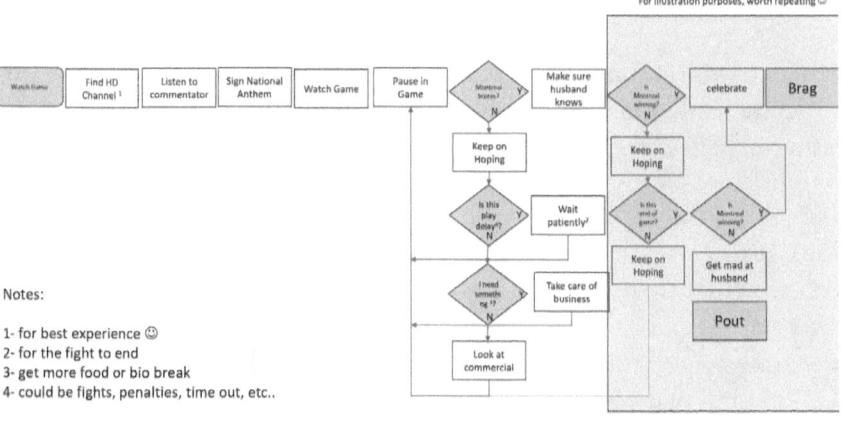

23

It seems to be true that the devil is in the details. The quality of these activities will influence our experience:

Type of Activities	Description	Example	Goal
Value-Added (VA)	The VA steps are only once and done right the first time The client wants it all the time Involves physical change Directly contributes to the results (emphasis is on the *do*—the action)	Depending on your perspective in this example, it could be goals (scores) or fights. I, personally, do not like to see fights; but over the years, I heard that for some, this was part of the experience. Does the client want it? As I go and see a hockey game, I expect every time that the teams will try and make goals. The transformation occurs when there is a goal. Making goals will influence the outcome of the game. Will your team win or not? By scoring, it directly affects the outcome.	It is important to optimize the VA!
Non-Value-Added (NVA) or Business Value (BA)	It is the glue is necessary, but it interrupts the flow of the value to the client. Required to do the Value-Added steps It is called the overhead	A great example of NVA steps are commercials. They would be considered NVA because they are required in order to get money to pay hockey players. At the same time, too many commercials would become a waste. In this category, I would dare to say fights. Some fights could be considered entertaining for some, but it interrupts the flow of the game. Again, too much could become a waste.	It is important *to minimize* the NVA!
Waste	Repetition of the value-added step (known as rework) Client does not want this. Is done to answer a perceived need Some represents errors, handoffs	As for waste activities, it could be very different for the person who is going there to see hockey, but only sees fights. The fights could become a waste. Penalties would be errors as it goes against the rules.	It is important *to eliminate* the waste!

Depending on one's expectations, the experience will be vastly different as we are all different in our perspectives. There are no right or wrong answers.

Now, how do you know you should be doing something? You need to look at the timeliness of your process—basically, the *process time (PT)*, or the actual time spent on processing a request (touch time), and the *cycle time (CT)*, or the end-to-end time, from the request of a client to the time where the service is delivered. It is the difference between CT and PT that equals the potential for improvements.

In the hockey example above, it takes sixty minutes to play a hockey game (three times twenty minutes), but end-to-end could potentially take three hours (depends on if you are traveling). The process maps show all the activities that are to be considered.

We saw that each of them were either value-added (VA), non-value-added (NVA), or waste. If it takes three weeks for me to get my benefit, why is that? It might take minutes to verify my identity and input information in the computer. Why does it, sometimes, take so much time? What are the steps that are required to achieve this result? Once the steps are identified, we need to understand the reason why we are doing them.

Why Do We Do What We Do?

WHY, WHY, WHY, WHY, WHY . . .
MY FAVORITE QUESTION.

You might want to understand the underlying conditions of why things are the way they are. A good root cause analysis will provide you with some answers. Just like the information provided in this chapter, there are several ways to analyse a situation. Use the one that you are most comfortable with; my preference is to ask *why*. Why? Why? What are you trying to achieve?

In my experience, this step is the most missed. Why is that? you ask. Because when we ask *why*, we uncover some of the hard truth in an organization. I got several tips that tell me if I am at the root of an issue.

- Does it explain the past, and does it hurt?
- Is it measurable?
- Are we still talking about communication and training? If yes, then it means it's something else!

I know that I like to eat at the restaurant more times than I should. One of the consequences of eating at a restaurant on a regular basis is that it is expensive. If I do a root cause analysis of this situation, it could go this way.

Symptom: I am spending too much money on food.

Why?
- I got nothing to eat.
- I am too tired to cook.

Why?
- It is easier to oder out.
- It is faster than cooking.

Why?
- I do not know what I want to eat.
- I did not planned my food this week.

Why?
- I got distracted by the kids (yep, good reason).
- I did not planned our activities.

Why?
- I did not take the time to plan.
- I got busy with something else.

In the above example, the lack of planning is influencing me in spending too much money on food. It is a simplistic example that shows a couple of things.

One, I do not take the time to plan because I am doing something for someone else. I need to take the time for myself as well. Even planning meals for the week will take care of my family too. Unfortunately, this sounds true for me on so many levels. Second, the root cause is also usually something that is not in the same space and time of the symptoms. In this example, I would spend money on the restaurant on Wednesday because I did not plan on Sunday!

The lack of planning is measurable. I can see the impacts of this when I plan my meals and I do not spend money on the restaurant. I could even do an experiment to see if this root cause is true to me. I would plan my meals for four weeks and see the impact on my budget. This is a common example that demonstrated the steps of the suggested spoiler alert (see p.14).

At work, I remember we had applications that were not processed for months. I started to walk the floor and noticed that employees were doing a triage of applications. We received thousands of applications a year, and we were spending many hours and resources to count them and put them in categories. I was concerned because it was encouraging inappropriate behaviors. Employees would choose the easy files and leave the more complex ones on the side. This was a normal behavior because we were measuring the number of applications that employees would process in a day.

I started to question why we were doing things this way and got the answer: because we have always done it this way! Well, I got excited because I knew I was on to something. I questioned and questioned, until I found out the following: One year, we hired a bunch of students during the summer. We divided the applications to make sure they had the easiest one to do. That was ten years ago! Today, our employees have over twenty years of experience and are well versed in all types of applications. We stopped doing this triage, and the timeliness of the processing got better. The first files in were the first files out.

Why Should We Ask Why?

Because it affects the bottom line.

In the work I did over the years, I was able to save millions of dollars in processing to reinvest in the organization. This transformational work is hard work as it deals with real issues in the business. At the same time, it provides the best results. Today, I see work that I did in 2003 that is still implemented in 2022 and provides excellent results.

In my example with the restaurant, it will require me to carve out some time in my schedule to do the planning of my meals. It might hurt my schedule in the short term, but it would be benefit to my bank account and also my health.

Getting to the bottom of things also helps stop recurring crisis. It helps address issues that we have never been able to address and to get a handle on things. Over the years, I found this to be true for any type of service or product development. Management processes, like human resource management, information management, innovation development, etc., can all be mapped and analysed to improve their effectiveness and efficiency.

I would even challenge you to look at home; how do you do laundry? I can assure you there are ways to improve the way you are doing things. The enclosed banner provides you with one approach. If you surf the internet, you will see that there are numerous resources on process improvement.

The enclosed is your minimum requirement to have results to build over time. I found that I did not have to wait for the perfect time to do something. There is no perfect time. As long as I started,

I would create a foundation for the future. My guiding light was to involve people in everything I did.

I need to say a major thank you to Hammer and Company. Throughout the years, the process management perspective influenced my leadership style positively in many ways.

I would also recognize the contribution of the Institute for Citizen-Centred Service. The Citizens First series that started in 1998 inspired my interactions and leadership in the public service. It was my true north.

IMPROVEMENT APPROACH

1. Look at an activity in your world that brings you pain.
2. Evaluate it from a perspective of cost, quality, and flexibility in doing business, and timeliness of service.
3. Map out the steps that reflect the sequence of activities.
4. Look at the value that each brings.
5. Ask why, why, why, why, why, why, do the steps need to exist.
6. Determine how they can either be eliminated or refocussed to add more value.
7. Measure the whole thing.
8. Review your results.
9. Do some testing.
10. Roll-out.
11. Document your experience.
12. Repeat the whole process.

"*Note to Self*"
Learning Solutions

_____

_____

_____

_____

_____

_____

_____

_____

_____

EMPLOYEE PERSPECTIVE

Aren't Employees Just Paid to Do a Job?

I HEARD THIS TOO MANY TIMES, AND IF THEY ARE, THEN WE ARE MISSING A BIG OPPORTUNITY.

The employees play a critical role as they execute the process; they will influence the client satisfaction significantly (ICCS, January 2022). What happens if employees know that what they are doing is meaningful? What happens if they are having a bad day? What happens if the work conditions are less than ideal? Clients will live the impacts of the employee's day, which, in turn, will provide a good, bad, or ugly service experience.

The client experience will either be positive or suffer based on the interaction with the employees. Take a moment to reflect on how you can influence the work environment so that you have positive experiences with your clients.

Remember when you received a great service. Can you remember a time when you gave amazing service? How were you feeling? How did you treat your colleagues, your clients? Now, when you were not feeling optimal (happens to all of us), what was the difference in your service? What kind of comments did you get?

"Note to Self"
Learning Solutions

_____

_____

_____

_____

_____

_____

_____

_____

_____

As you can see, the employees' actions at work are most likely to determine the client experience. In short, the employees need to feel the love.

What Does Love Have to Do with It?

WHAT ARE YOU TALKING ABOUT, GIRL?
LOVE? THIS IS A BUSINESS BOOK.

When we think about employee wellness, I often hear about illness. In the work environment, we talked about depression, PTSD, burnouts, etc. This perspective looks at the issues and tries to manage the symptoms. This reactive approach focusses on managing the illness. In this model, we have little control of the situation; most leaders are not doctors or health professionals.

In my experience, it is very depressing to deal with only negative situations. My energy depletes rapidly when I do not have any control to help employees face difficult challenges. My aspiration is to create a work environment where employees can be the best version of themselves at work. I questioned myself repeatedly on what the existing opportunities to support this venture could be. What could I do to support employees to deal with their situation? As I mentioned in my introduction, I believe that work matters. My work has supported me towards an overall good health practice. What could I do for others?

Again, What Does Love Have to Do with It?

A SYSTEM VIEW OF WELLNESS.

I did some research that led me to a standard called Psychological Health and Safety in the Workplace. The Canadian Standard Association (CSA) and the Bureau de Normalisation du Québec (BNQ) developed the standard and released it in January 2013. It was developed with industry representatives, governments, employee assistance service providers, academia, and unions.

Thirteen workplace factors were developed and you can view them as best practices (see enclosed banner). These factors are organizational or systemic in nature and, if implemented, will yield a positive outcome. This means that we can influence these factors to create a healthy work environment. I was optimistic about this potential!

I was fortunate to be in contact with these factors in several of my roles in the federal public service. It was useful to identify some hazards in the workplace and related mitigation strategies. I assessed the health of my teams, divisions, and overall organization. Most of all these factors brought an element of control for my leaders and me.

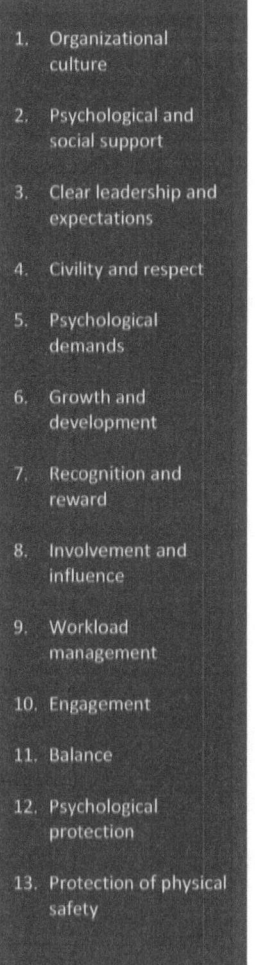

THIRTEEN FACTORS

1. Organizational culture
2. Psychological and social support
3. Clear leadership and expectations
4. Civility and respect
5. Psychological demands
6. Growth and development
7. Recognition and reward
8. Involvement and influence
9. Workload management
10. Engagement
11. Balance
12. Psychological protection
13. Protection of physical safety

They can directly influence and support employees, which, in turn, creates value for the organization. The Institute for Citizen-Centred Service states it eloquently: "The equation is simple: When employees are engaged in their work, they provide better services, which has a positive impact on citizen trust and confidence in government." (ICCS, January 2022)

When you think about it, this can be viewed as common sense. In some of our practices, we might forget this important relationship. What can we do then? What is under our control?

If you look closely at the thirteen factors, you will notice that you control all of them to a certain degree. In my opinion, the degree will be dependent on your amount of control in the workplace. We should all care because….

> By addressing [the thirteen workplace factors] effectively has the potential to positively impact the workplace and employee mental health, psychological 'safety, and participation, which, in turn, affects productivity. (CSA n.d.)

I also was able to observe through my own results of the Public Service Employee Survey that the overall trust in leaders has positively increased over the years. You want to play a bit with these factors? At the end of this chapter, you will find a word search match with definitions and examples of each of these categories. Have fun!

The exercise gave you examples of activities that are in the workplace to support a healthy work environment. Another way to look at it is from the lens of different committees at work.

Over the years, I have heard leaders question the values of committees. When done properly, it can contribute to the overall well-being of the organization. Here are some examples:

- The Health and Safety committee supports both physical safety and psychological protection.

- The Employment Equity and Diversity committee contributes to civility and respect, engagement, and employee involvement.
- The Training and Learning committee to have a focus attention on growth and development.

I could go on and on; the key point here is that both employees and leaders co-create the work environment. These factors are a platform that encourages such a relationship. Remember our graphic? Employee actions impact clients and organizational results and outcomes.

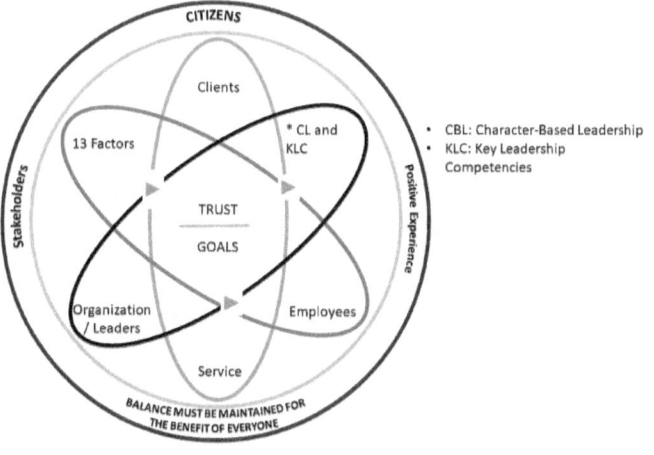

As you can see, we (all employees) are part of the solution, either by respecting our core values, participating in the workplace, or taking care of ourselves. I found that in order to sustain the efforts over time, I needed to find a reason why my work contributes to my personal growth. At the end of the day, we are all working for a reason, either to provide value at home or to provide for our family or personal fulfillments. Everyone makes a difference in the lives of people. This is why as employees; we need to take care of ourselves.

Who Does What Again?

WE ARE ALL PART OF THE SOLUTIONS.

Before I go further, I need to acknowledge that we have a key role to play as employees in organizations. We are all participants to create a positive, healthy work environment. In every organization, there are values, cultures, and behaviors that are expected. As an example, in the public service, we have expected behaviors that are part of our Values and Ethics Code for the Public Sector-Canada.ca (tbs-sct.gc.ca) which is part of our conditions of employment.

If you do not have a prescribed direction, I am sharing my practices, which over the years, I have found to be successful in maintaining positive work relationships with my supervisors, my colleagues, and my employees:

- ✓ I have the responsibility to speak up when I see something that is just not right.
- ✓ I need to participate in creating the conditions for success.
- ✓ I need to take care of myself.
- ✓ I need to bring my ideas forward and be open to change.
- ✓ I need also to be civil with my colleagues and supervisors.
- ✓ I need to honor the past.

You will notice that these behaviors are closely linked to the employee responsibilities under the occupational health safety practices (ESDC n.d.).

Participating in a healthy work environment is essential for all of us. Being safe at work also means being healthy, hence occupational health and safety. I heard several times that health is the condition to bring you to work, and safety is the condition to bring you back home. Let's expand on this a bit more.

What about Our Health?

Swarbrick's (2006) approach to wellness highlights key elements, which are emotional, social, spiritual, environmental, physical, occupational, financial, and intellectual wellness.

I would encourage you to evaluate each dimension against your own practices.

"*Note to Self*"
Learning Solutions

_____

_____

_____

_____

_____

_____

_____

_____

_____

Please remember that they are all interrelated. I already established earlier that our actions influence the expected outcome in our lives and at work. They directly affect client satisfaction as well as our own happiness. I actually did a jeopardy game to reinforce the message that we need to take care of ourselves individually, if we want to bring the best version of ourselves to work.

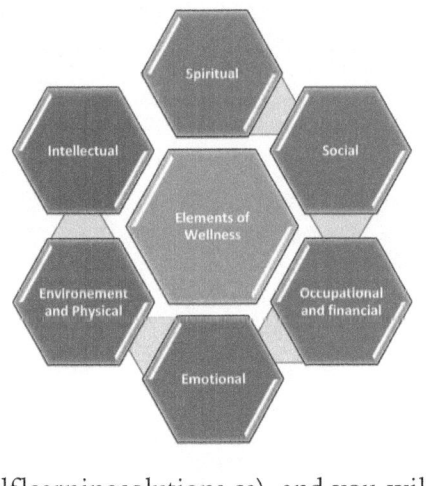

Please go to my website (notetoselflearningsolutions.ca), and you will have a version of it. We are fortunate to live in a time where there is a wealth of resources on these elements either in great authors or on the internet. Have fun exploring these topics.

In this space, there are no wrong answers. My advice is to go to what gives you energy and makes you feel the love and the beauty of this world.

I am inspired by books I read. One author that speaks to my soul is Robin Sharma. Based on his teachings, I developed my own practice. I wake up a couple of hours before work time. My routine starts with thirty minutes' exercise, followed by a nice shower. I love to give myself thirty minutes to meditate, reflect, or read some passages in a book. Once I feel that I can face the world (normally after a good cup of coffee), I start my workday.

This approach ensures that I bring the best version of myself to work. Recently I started a new mandate and my schedule was off track. It took me a while, but I found new ways to get the energy and creativity to write a book, work in a full-time demanding job, and be a good friend, mother, and wife! It is a juggling act, and at the same time, when I am centered, a very fulfilling one.

Reminder: As you read these chapters, you might come to the conclusion that you are out of balance. Please reach out to a friend, family, or a medical professional to discuss your situation. You are not alone. The Canadian Mental Health Association provides strategies to get help for yourself or someone you know. In Canada, CMHA National (cmha.ca) is a great resource, and in USA, (www. mhanational.org).

I Want to Ride My Bicycle

LET'S GO FOR A RIDE.

In order to bring together the thirteen workplace factors and the eight elements, I like to use the example of a bicycle. It shows the relationship between individual and organizational wellness. The front wheel can be the organizational wellness with the thirteen factors. The spokes of the wheels need to be aligned for the organization to be psychologically safe.

For example, I need to manage the workload effectively if I am going to encourage my employees to have a work-life balance. If I encourage employees not to send emails at night, I also need to have a level of comfort that they can do their work on a normal working day. If not, there will be conflicting messages that could lead to stress for all. The messages between these two spokes (workload management and balance) need to be congruent. I often hear that management speaks from both sides of their mouths when two conflicting messages are shared with employees. In time, this conflict might undermine some leadership practices.

In the back of your bicycle, you have the eight elements of individual wellness. Again, the spokes need to be balanced to be centered and bring the best version of yourself at work.

Too often, I did not sleep well at night and went to work. During those days, I needed to be extra careful in my interactions with people. I needed to make sure that my lack of sleep was not sending my mind into overdrive. You know, when you always know that person had bad intentions, and you discover it when your mind is making all kinds of end-of-the-world scenarios. A trigger for me to know that I am not my best version at work? Everyone is evil. Obviously, everyone cannot be bad. This is when I check myself and decide to take a break and come back to the issue later.

My message here is that at the very least, the doctors were right: eat well, sleep well, and oh, yes, that one—exercise well every day. Get your body moving to feel the energy of life. At a minimum, having these three foundations help manage the rest of the spokes in your bicycle.

It is both wheels together that create the conditions for the bicycle to move forward. Think about it, can you really be your best version if you do not trust your colleagues or your boss? Can you be really present if you did not sleep all night or felt sluggish? If you can, cool, but most cannot. Now, are you able to keep your balance on your bike? If not, check your wheels. If you are not sure on how you are doing and need guidance, please keep on reading.

How Do I Know What I Do Not Know?

Good question!

If you are not sure where to go next or how well you are doing, I will refer you to the Mental Health Continuum that was developed by the Department of National Defense in Canada (see graphic from the Mental Health Commission in 2017). This model is powerful. As you look at your symptoms, it empowers you to also consider some actions to support your well-being.

I remember a time when I was so lost in my own reality that I did not know that I was in a vicious cycle and hurting myself. Actually, I thought I was handling everything very well. I was extremely productive at work. I was going through a separation, but I was OK dealing with it; I had it all together to a point that I crashed. I am not saying that these symptoms mean everyone crashes, but I am saying that I was unconscious and doing a bunch of stuff, being busy but not taking care of myself. Some of my habits were also questionable, such as liking too much wine. If I would have looked at this chart, I was in the "ill" column (far right). It is only when I had professional help that I got better. I took the time to understand what I was living through, and actually, this saved my life. Later on, I got to recognize the symptoms, and I was able to be proactive in dealing with it.

The other perspective I like about this model is that you can be in a reacting zone and go back to a healthy place. As I look at my day, depending on how I respond to an event, I can fluctuate. When I do, I have activities to help me better cope with my day.

Again, this model does not replace medical advice. It might help to support you to be proactive in getting advice or even help you maintain a healthy lifestyle. I like to use the Mental Health Continuum and the activities, like various signs, in the workplace.

If I show you a green or red square with a cross, you will know automatically that it represents first aid station.

If you see a red octagon, you will know there is a stop sign.

You do not have to think; your brain registers what you are looking for. For me, the Mental Health Continuum is the same thing; the different areas represent zones of caution that I should pay attention. The activities are what I need to do to redress or maintain a zone. I just need to review my emotions or behaviors.

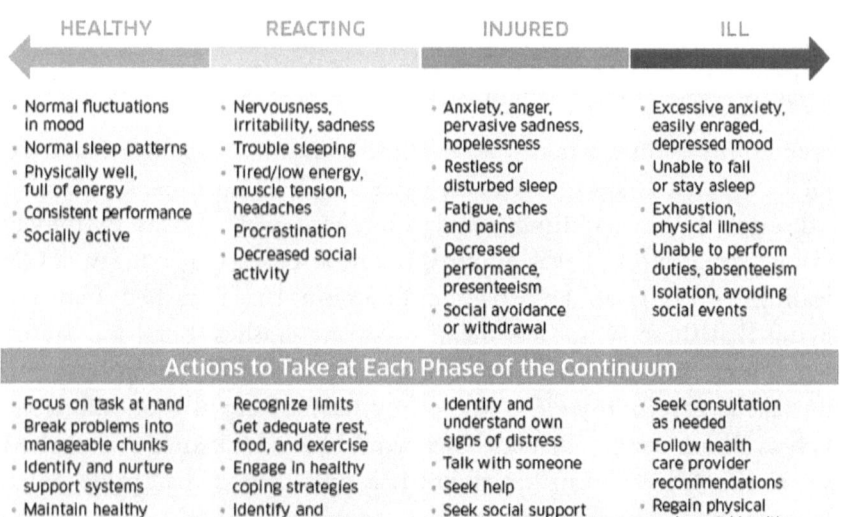

MENTAL HEALTH CONTINUUM MODEL

HEALTHY	REACTING	INJURED	ILL
• Normal fluctuations in mood • Normal sleep patterns • Physically well, full of energy • Consistent performance • Socially active	• Nervousness, irritability, sadness • Trouble sleeping • Tired/low energy, muscle tension, headaches • Procrastination • Decreased social activity	• Anxiety, anger, pervasive sadness, hopelessness • Restless or disturbed sleep • Fatigue, aches and pains • Decreased performance, presenteeism • Social avoidance or withdrawal	• Excessive anxiety, easily enraged, depressed mood • Unable to fall or stay asleep • Exhaustion, physical illness • Unable to perform duties, absenteeism • Isolation, avoiding social events

Actions to Take at Each Phase of the Continuum

• Focus on task at hand • Break problems into manageable chunks • Identify and nurture support systems • Maintain healthy lifestyle	• Recognize limits • Get adequate rest, food, and exercise • Engage in healthy coping strategies • Identify and minimize stressors	• Identify and understand own signs of distress • Talk with someone • Seek help • Seek social support instead of withdrawing	• Seek consultation as needed • Follow health care provider recommendations • Regain physical and mental health

I will reinforce that as you read these words or look at this chart, and it could wake up all kinds of emotions.

Please take care of yourself and reach out to someone, either a friend, family, or medical professional. I will repeat the following information: The Canadian Mental Health Association provides a strategies to get help for you or someone you know. In Canada,

CMHA National (cmha.ca) is a great resource, and in USA, Mental Health America (www.mhanational.org).

In a team environment, this tool has the potential to demystify psychological practices at work. In the past, it enabled me to have check-in with employees. Just a quick conversation: "Hey, you want to have a coffee?" "I have seen that you changed, you seem sad about something?"

I also used it at the organizational level with a panel of discussion with my senior leaders and colleagues. We shared on how we use the model in our every day life. There is lots of potential to make this model your own. See enclosed example, how would you use it?

Individual

- Self-assessment
- Perform check-ins
- Proactively identify activities to help manage through each stage
- What are some of your activities?

Team

- Focus conversations on where we are as a team on the continuum
- Enable proactive conversations and sharing activities to support staying healthy
- Share stories on techniques that helped survived and grow from challenges
- What are some of your teams' activities?

Organizational

- Determine psychological hazards in the workplace
- Normalize the conversation on psychological health
- Supports leaders in a common language and a tool to support the duty to inquire.
- What are other organizational activities?

At the end of the day, it is your responsibility to take care of yourself; no one can do it for you. We are humans taking care, directly or indirectly, of other humans. This is a big responsibility. I hope the above offers you some ideas for success. It does not have to be complicated. Just take one thing at a time and build on your experience.

Your leaders can also help play a role in creating the conditions for a psychologically safe environment. Let's take a look.

Thank you to all that participated in the creation of the Psychological Health and Safety in the Workplace Standard. The Standard gives me a sense of control over my environment and the confidence to be able to do something. A big thank you as well to the creators of the Mental Health Continuum. This tool puts wellness in the hands of the one that owns it . . . me!

Just for Fun

LET'S PLAY A LITTLE BIT.

Search for those thirteen factors.

Your mission, if you choose to take it, is two-fold: (1) to review all the factors and fill in the missing words, then (2) go in the puzzle area and find the words. For ease of reference, the eighteen words are identified below. Have fun!

Please note that the definitions and examples for each of the factors were quoted or inspired by Guarding Minds at Work's "Suggested Actions and Resources" (guardingmindsatwork.ca).

Factor 1: Organizational _____

It is a mix of *norms, values, beliefs, meanings, and expectations* that group members hold in common and that they use as behavioural and problem-solving cues.

Examples:

- "The way things are done around here."
- Evidence on how the other twelve factors are implemented.
- Conflict is addressed respectfully.
- There is a trust and camaraderie within the unit.
- Diversity in thinking and backgrounds.

Factor 2: Psychological and Social Support

It comprises all supportive _____ available at work, either with co-workers or supervisors. It refers to the degree of social and emotional integration and trust among co-workers and supervisors.

Examples:

- Reduce stigma
- Offer mental health education
- Help employees to have coping strategies
- Share services internal and external to the organization
- Peer support programs
- Accommodations for individual requirements

Factor 3: Clear _____ and _____

It is present in an environment in which *leadership is effective* and provides sufficient support that helps workers know what they need to do, explains how their work contributes to the organization, and discusses the nature and expected outcomes of impending changes.

Examples:

- Clear roles and responsibilities
- Conflict is addressed respectfully
- Timely two-way communication
- Performance feedback

Factor 4: _____ and Respect

It is present in a work environment where workers *are respectful and considerate* in their interactions with one another, as well as with customers, clients, and the public.

Examples:

- Clarify what is acceptable/unacceptable behaviors
- Support for difficult conversations (Informal Conflict Resolution)

- Teach mindfulness practices
- Engage all teams to develop a code of ethics
- Use team tools to explore different ideas (de Bono's six thinking hats).

Factor 5: Psychological Competencies and Demands

Guarding Minds at Work defines psychological competencies and demands as a work environment where there is _____ between employees' interpersonal and emotional competencies, their job skills, and the position they hold.

Examples:

- Let employees explore internal position (job shadowing, coaching)
- Build stronger teams
- Develop emotional intelligence in the organization
- Do a personal value assessment ("Evidence-Based Actions for Psychological Competencies and Demands" (workplacestrategiesformentalhealth.com)

Factor 6: _____ and Development

It is present in a work environment where workers receive encouragement and support in the development of their *interpersonal, emotional, and job skills.*

Examples:

- Explore how employees want to receive _____ see quick survey: "Putting Growth And Development on the Agenda: Creating Awareness" (mediresource.com)
- Areas to develop growth: skills, communication, leadership, performance, emotional intelligence, collaboration, innovation, ethics, and knowledge
- Make action plan: easy wins and long-term goals

Factor 7: Recognition and Reward

It is present in a work environment where there is appropriate _____ and appreciation of workers' efforts in a fair and timely manner.

Examples:

- Make it personal. Identify your preference: frequent/monthly? On quality of work/efforts and attitude? In public/private? In writing/oral? Individual/team?
- Provide opportunities
- Offer beyond-the-call-of-duty perks
- Facilitate peer-to-peer recognition
- Recognise people's passions
- Embrace gamification
- Make accomplishments public

Factor 8: Involvement and _____

It is present in a work environment where workers are *included* in discussions about how their work is done and how important decisions are made.

Examples:

- Identify the decisions that cannot consider your opinion. These decisions are related to:
  o Human rights
  o Regulations
  o Quality assurance
  o Business decisions requiring confidentiality due to third-party involvements, investments, or major purchases
- Identify areas where you want more influence: scheduling, resources, equipment, planning, evaluation, innovation, or procedures
- Tiger teams, process improvement initiatives
- Dual responsibility between leader (to listen) and employee (to participate)

Factor 9: _____ **Management**

It is present in a work environment where assigned tasks and responsibilities can be accomplished successfully *within the time available.*

Examples:

- Set clear and reasonable expectations
- Identify what control and not and mitigation strategies
- Prioritizing
- Discuss workplace interruptions and mitigation strategies
- Consider non-remunerative perks to encourage employees
- Identify the workload stress-related causes

Factor 10: _____

It is present in a work environment where workers enjoy and feel connected to their work and where they feel *motivated* to do their job well.

Examples:

- Evidence of engagement:
  - Energized: Using our strengths in specific opportunities, like facilitating a team meeting
  - Interested: Learning opportunities that help me improve at my job
  - Proud: Volunteering during work hours with my team
  - Dedicated: Getting feedback from clients about how my work helps them
  - Eager: Adding fun activities to our workday
- Tiger team, process improvement projects, simulations, lab-pilots
- Gamification
- Coaching
- Committee and project work
- Show results, such as _____
- Performance management, provide feedback

Factor 11: _____ (or Work-Life Harmony)

It is present in a work environment where there is acceptance of the need for a sense of _____between the demands of personal life, family, and work.

Examples:

- Lead by example and take breaks, vacations, etc.
- Regular check-in on workload management progress
- Adopt practices that support harmony, such as limit after hour emails, especially in weekends.
- Share home life stories, personal projects, pets, etc.

Factor 12: Psychological _____

Workplace _____ safety is demonstrated when workers feel able to put themselves on the line, ask questions, seek feedback, report mistakes and problems, or propose a new idea without fearing negative consequences to themselves, their job, or their career.

Examples:

- Diversity is encouraged by sharing ideas
- Psychological hazards are identified, communicated, and mitigated
- Resources for employees are available
- Situations are timely dealt with respect and dignity

Factor 13: Protection of Physical Safety

It is present when a worker's psychological, as well as physical _____, is protected from hazards and risks related to the worker's physical environment.

Examples:

- Employees are trained on how to deal with hazards
- There is a health and safety management system in place
- Regular follow-ups are communicated on hazards

- The workplace respect existing legislative requirements

Now that you have found the words, let's continue the fun and find the words. Track your time. How much time did it take you?

I suggest using the highlighter to track your success. Draw and choose your preference.

Feedback
Social Interactions
Engagement
Civility
Leadership
Culture
Balance
Good fit
Acknowledgement
Protection
Harmony
Psychological
Expectations
Growth
Motivation
Influence
Safety
Workload

```
O  L  A  T  T  O  H  W  N  A  S  C  L  Y  U  Y  C  F  J
A  P  N  P  D  W  A  V  A  L  O  M  W  O  T  E  S  U  I
W  T  P  D  P  O  R  H  L  C  C  W  U  R  B  X  H  D  O
A  P  S  T  C  R  M  O  E  D  I  K  O  H  I  P  O  E  H
C  N  Y  G  N  K  O  K  A  R  A  V  H  C  O  E  H  C  I
K  A  C  M  R  L  N  T  D  T  L  C  I  U  D  C  N  P  U
N  W  H  C  E  O  Y  I  E  K  I  A  Q  L  A  T  L  V  M
O  A  O  Y  N  A  W  P  R  C  N  C  Y  T  I  A  A  P  Z
W  P  L  Y  G  D  C  T  S  C  T  V  O  U  D  T  N  N  N
L  H  O  D  A  O  O  A  H  N  E  I  O  R  D  I  Y  O  T
E  T  G  G  G  C  F  I  B  R  N  O  E  P  O  S  M  D
D  O  I  K  E  O  H  E  P  D  A  F  B  N  A  N  C  A  I
G  R  C  A  M  O  O  E  N  C  C  L  B  E  Y  S  E  Y  R
E  I  A  K  E  D  S  D  R  E  T  U  A  V  B  U  V  P  P
M  A  L  C  N  F  E  B  P  Y  I  E  M  N  L  I  H  C  N
E  K  M  O  T  I  V  A  T  I  O  N  A  A  C  S  C  H  O
N  C  R  I  D  T  A  C  G  P  N  C  S  A  F  E  T  Y  A
T  B  B  A  A  C  E  K  P  S  S  E  K  N  N  A  A  G  T
H  D  S  O  C  T  G  P  T  H  E  D  M  I  S  O  N  A  A
```

Please note that the answer sheet can be found at notetoselflearningsolutions.ca

_____

_____

_____

_____

_____

_____

_____

_____

ORGANIZATIONAL PERSPECTIVE

Are You Awake Yet?

THE FUN IS JUST STARTING.

Now before you fall asleep just by reading the title of this chapter, really think about why you should read this chapter. Especially if you do not have a formal leadership role, why read it? Because it might demystify some of management's actions that you saw and could not explain throughout your career. Maybe you can also help by bringing your perspective to the table and being part of the solutions.

Why should you care about the organization? At its smallest expression, it helps to pay the bills! Point!

The power of a business is to create value for its clients and employees. As we saw in our graphic (Atom), it is a symbiotic relationship. When I think about the organizational perspective, I think to safeguard the integrity that we have in the system, which is delegated to its management structure.

I have always had high expectations for leaders; the consequences of our decisions can have long standing impacts. As a formal leader, I have been trusted by authorities to act in the best interest of taxpayers (shareholders). It is my duty to be a good steward of these assets.

In the following sections, I will describe some fundamental attributes from my learnings to maintain this integrity.

What Gets Measured Gets Done, Really?

No joke, it does.

In Dr. Cohn's words, "Metrics drive behaviors" (2015). Since I have done root cause analysis of many processes, I soon realized that what gets measured gets done. If we do not measure the right things, it can encourage inappropriate behaviors. As an example, if I only measure the number of processed claims, well, I get processed claims. The quality of these claims might suffer.

I would challenge you to ask why. Why? Why? Most likely one of the key variables will be that you do not have enough time to accomplish all your tasks. Consequently, you will most likely do what is the most important to your performance metrics, which will demonstrate your achievements.

I learned to look at the system as a whole and questioned each performance measure that came my way. The measurement system can be quite complex, but I like to keep it simple. As I look at a process, organization, etc., I question myself on what it is they are trying to achieve and how I know the objectives are achieved. Then I put these measures (no matter the project) under these gates:

- Are they accurate? (Explain what's being measured.)
- Are they objectives? (Clear—not subject to interpretation.)
- Are they easy to understand?
- Are they easy to collect?
- Are they just in time?
- What is the behavior being encouraged? Is it harmless? Does it support appropriate behaviors?

Let's take a moment to reflect on these. If I measure only the number of files to be processed, yes, the right thing is measured (files). Files are objectives and easy to understand (it is a number). Most likely, easy to collect as they are inputted into a system. Hopefully, there is a process to collect this information in a timely manner.

In my experience, it falls short to pass the last gate. We have to wait weeks and months to see our results. In my book, the most important question is, What is the behavior it is encouraging? In order to encourage the quality of the work, we would need a measure of performance that speaks about success rate or resolution at first point of contact and the like.

This is easier said than done. Most metrics are already published and approved by high levels of the organization. Therefore, as a leader, the challenge is to complement the set of measures you need to report on to ensure you have the whole picture of your organization.

I will use another example to bring this point forward. In my leadership role, I get measured on program results and for creating a psychologically safe environment. What would happen if I only managed on program results? I would ensure that all our targets are met. I would ensure that my measurement system provides me with output on my key accountabilities on a regular basis. This in itself is good sound management.

Let's look at another scenario: I would like to understand my client experience; which would be the best indicator?

a. Timeliness of a service
b. Number of client requests
c. Number and type of request resolved
d. None of the above, we do not need to measure this. It is my company and I will do what I want.

Proposed Solution and Rationale

The premise of this book is that a quality service is a balance between clients, employees and the organization. Therefore, option *D* in this scenario is not viable for me.

Gates	Option A	Option B	Option C
Accurate	X	X	X
Objective	X	X	X
Easy to Understand	Potentially (if simple)	X	X
Easy to Collect	X	X	Harder
Just in Time	X	X	X
Behavior	High	Medium	Low

At face value, option B could be the best one, but it would provide only one dimension of the client experience (i.e., their request). Did we answer their concerns? We do not know.

Then option A (one I see often) is also important in assessing the quality of the service but by itself can introduce inappropriate behaviors (only processing files without taking into account the quality), which (for me) is unacceptable.

Now option C would give me the number of clients that contacted us and the type of services we provided to resolve their issues. This one looks like it would be harder to collect but yield fewer behavioral issues.

As you can see, there are no perfect solutions. What would be your answer? Just on the above indicators, I would say that option A and option C would provide a good understanding of my client experience. I would have the same amount of time my employees spend in working with clients to resolve their issues. But wait . . . is it complete?

Remember, in my leadership role, I get measured on program results and for creating a psychologically safe environment.

It would not be that simple; we mentioned that employees influence the quality of the client services. Then I would need a picture of that relationship. Are my employees courteous? If not, then I would need to do a root cause analysis.

This example shows that taken individually, the indicators can do harm. I only showed the client and organizational perspectives at this point. When I add the dimension of employees by creating a psychologically safe environment, then I need to ensure that my employees are willing participants at work.

In the previous chapter, we saw that there are thirteen factors to create conditions for a healthy work environment. Well, in my leadership role, now I need to attend to employees' well-being as well as program results. It is not just about the client and employees; leaders play a critical role.

I could have gone into the sophistication of the data collection, retention, protection, etc. for the analysis. There are many complexities in a measurement system. The above scenario is for illustration purposes only. My key message is beware of what gets measured because it gets done! If it is only numbers, then we will encourage employees to find ways to show numbers.

In this scenario, we would get only a partial view of the client experience. In order to understand fully, we would also need to understand their relationship with our employees.

What Happens When You Are
Not Paying Attention?

THINGS GO OUT OF WACK.

This organizational perspective for me is essential to creating value for shareholders. In the public service, this is our taxpayers. In order to stay relevant, we need to see our contribution. If I did not pay attention, I found that it was easy to revert back to bureaucratic behaviors. These non-value work activities can create delays and errors that affect the integrity of the system.

There are two types of errors. First, one that affects service delivery. For example, I forgot to ask a question to determine eligibility. I need to contact the client a second time. This action might create delays in processing the request.

Second, one that affects the integrity of a system. For example, if I put the email address of a client in the wrong file. Then I could potentially share private information with the wrong client. As you can see, workplace actions matter. Therefore, we need some indicators that speak to the health of the business.

Over the years, I measured the effectiveness and efficiency through questionnaires and surveys to my staff as I found I was getting direct information. The public service also has regular surveys to its employees. Lately, I have been using Guarding Minds at Work (www.guardingmindsatwork.ca) survey on the thirteen factors for a psychologically safe work environment. This approach provided a picture for each unit under my responsibility on some of the leadership practices experienced by employees. It provided a roadmap to my leaders in order for them to action areas of concern.

I also played with the questionnaire by segregating the perspective of employees and leaders. I was positively surprised to find that I am getting a similar perspective from both employees. Leaders are reflecting actual employee concerns with minimal distortion. Consequently, my trust in the leaders increased.

This attention to measures is the influence of process management on me, which led me to the necessity to have a balanced approach to measurement. Early in my career, I was introduced to the Kaplan Norton Balance Scorecard, which I appreciated the approach to view the organization, as the vision is at its core and influence all the decisions.

At the same time, the Treasury Board Secretariat introduced the management accountability framework (MAF) early in my career. I was intrigued by its potential and its elegant simplicity.

Why Are Measures Important, Especially in Management?

Did I say what gets measured gets done?

In the perspective of oversights, the federal departments are accountable to the Treasury Board Secretariat (TBS) on areas of concern in any given year.

> The management accountability framework (MAF) is a tool used by the Treasury Board of Canada Secretariat (TBS) to monitor the management performance of federal departments and agencies. ("Management Accountability Framework," www. canada.ca)

But it could be so much more. I remember when I was first exposed to the MAF. I just thought it was brilliant. Even in doing my master's in business administration, I researched it and put it against some of the best practices of the time, and it was standing its own ground. Over the years, it has influenced the way I look at organizations. For me, it was the Kaplan version for the public sector.

As we look at the characteristics of a high performing organization and the elements of the MAF (see table next page), one can see the strength of the framework. It could serve as a roadmap for leaders across the public service.

High Performance Characteristics	Management Accountability Framework
1. Organizational design includes cross-functional teams and horizontal information sharing	Links to people (employee engagement)
2. Strategy link to vision and goals and clarity of direction both in short and long term	Links to governance, direction, and vision to results
3. Process are designed and have right measures; continuous learning and interactive communication	Balance service delivery and risk management Financial, stewardship, and accountability
4. Technology is flexible	Citizen-focused service that is supported by technology
5. Leadership inspire people, has integrity, uses coaching and listening skills to support employees in learning, and is committed to the organization and employees	Public service values; people component of the MAF
6. Individuals and roles are focused on learning and can-do attitudes; safe and secure environment	Learning, innovation, and change management
7. Empowers a culture focused on performance and core values that is open and trustworthy	Learning, innovation, and change management Public service values (Code of Value & Ethics)
8. The organization focuses on understanding the external environment by having a stakeholder focus, monitor the marketplace, and create value-adding work.	Policy and program development based on client requirements

Table: High Performance Organization and the MAF (Lemay 2009)

Table: High Performance Organization and the MAF (Lemay 2009)

If you review the information provided by TBS, you will notice that the process is the same if you are a big or small department. These are the criteria on which you will get assessed. In itself, this approach provides a sense of comfort of knowing that we are all treated in the same manner. It looks at the business from end to end and creates interoperability between functions. This is where I got excited! I see this potential.

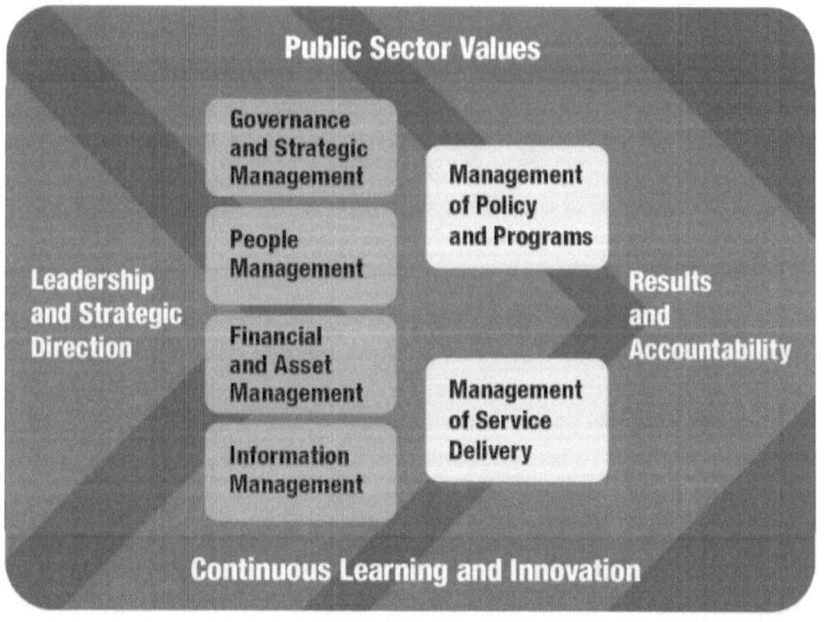

Source: MAFDiagram.jpg (1230 × 886) (atlas101.ca)

The above picture shows a summary of the MAF. I relate to it in the form of a story that speaks of the categories while using the traffic lights.

It starts with leadership and strategic direction. Are you having the appropriate vision/mission to achieve the results you require? If not, this is a showstopper! You need to stop what you are doing and revisit your actions (thus the red light).

In the earlier foundation chapter, I mentioned the importance of knowing what you want to achieve at the individual and organizational level. This is essential as you will measure and get the results that you are aiming for.

Then you might want to exercise caution in your policies for program development as well as service delivery (yellow light). The development of these needs are to be aligned with the clients' expectations, not just for today but also for tomorrow.

We saw earlier the relationship between client expectations and service delivery; this is also true for providing the appropriate programs and policy suites. The public servant will implement what is being designed at the policy and program level.

When the practices in place reflect continuous leadership with governance, strategic considerations, people and financial management, as well as sound information management practices, then all systems are a go (green light). If these processes are plagued with non-value-added activities, it will interfere with getting the results you want. The trick is to find this balance between the required steps to do the work, oversight and having confidence that the employees will do their work.

In order to ensure that the system is working properly, there is a need for regular check-ins. The continuous process of improvement of learning and innovating will ensure that the public service remains relevant. I dedicated the next chapter to this question.

The values in the public sector are also important. They provide us with a guidepost to behave. In our workplace action matters graphic, we see that leaders' behaviors directly influence the client and employee experience. This is why having a model to follow is instrumental, and this is why the MAF could be so much more. It can explain the importance of managing in the public service to all leaders.

My work in this space is ongoing. I still need to have more experience with the MAF. My goal is to make it real for leaders. If you have something to share with me on this topic, please do. I am interested in hearing your thoughts (notetoselflearningsolutions.ca). In the meantime, I want to share another aspect of the organizational perspective. The measurement system will give me what I do, but *how* I do it also matters, especially in a leadership role.

What about How We Do Things? You Ask

Key leadership competencies is the how.

Over the years, I learned that leadership is a discipline, and it is learnable. It no longer belongs to those charismatic leaders we see on TV. It is my experience that by consciously attending to one's competency and character, one can be effective and efficient in its leadership practices. These are models to aspire.

The government of Canada adopted that the key leadership competencies (KLC) are the norm for effective leadership expectations. The Treasury Board expects that

> The key leadership competencies (KLC) define the behaviours expected of Canada's Public Service leaders. This competency profile informs executives on how to lead, and serves as the fundamental basis for selection, learning and development, and performance and talent management of executives. ("Key Leadership Competencies" www.canada.ca, December 12, 2021)

As mentioned, KLC is used for staffing, performance management, and learning as well as talent management. Leaders are expected to demonstrate behaviours in the following six competency areas:

Create Vision and Strategy: This is your ability to demonstrate how everything is linked together. How does the vision of the organization link to the work you are performing? It goes beyond your own work by looking externally at the economic, political, and social environments. It balances that external and internal view for the benefit of citizens. It also supports clear leadership and expectations moving forward.

Mobilize People: This is what we traditionally think of human resource management with the emphasis on two-way communication and engagement. It speaks to leading by example and demonstrates how your personal vision motivates you to achieve results. How are you focused on performance excellence? It provides the conditions for employees to grow and develop as well as to be involved in the workplace.

Uphold Integrity and Respect: The example on page 73 provides you with an excellent perspective on the importance of this competency. The demonstration of this competency can result in an increase in civility and respect in the workplace as well as a psychologically safe work environment.

Collaborate with Partners and Stakeholders: In this competency, we find the notion of civility and respect by considering numerous perspectives and arriving at a consensus. It brings an enterprise view to the solutions as it considers the organization from end to end. Furthermore, this collaboration is acknowledged and recognized by all (you and your teams, partners, etc.).

Promote Innovation and Guide Change: This competency requires the most courage and requires that we take an intelligent risk approach to the issues in our environment. Leading by example in this space is essential, as it influences the organizational culture. The way we engage in managing mistakes, failures, or perceived errors will give the message if we have a risk-adverse culture or a growth approach to support our employees. Our behaviors will speak louder than our words.

Achieve Results: At the end of the day, we are here to provide value for our clients and taxpayers (shareholders). How proactive are you in adjusting your plans and respecting your priorities? Do your results only talk about one dimension of your mandate, like productivity, or are you also speaking about employee and client satisfaction? How are you managing your workloads? Do you accept responsibility for your actions and decisions, or are you blaming something else? Taking responsibility for your decisions as a leader is essential to show employees that you will support them and create a safe environment to learn. Measuring more than one dimension of your results will also permit employees to have a work-life harmony.

The execution of these competencies is closely related to the thirteen factors discussed in the preceding chapter. I already started to provide examples in my descriptions of the KLCs.

I would challenge you to read each competency again with the thirteen factors; you will see dimensions that crossover. For example, using all the KLC's influence, the organizational culture, if I mobilize people, I will automatically involve people, engage them, respect diversity, growth, and development, etc. I challenge you to unpack these competencies with the factors; one enables the other.

"*Note to Self*"
Learning Solutions

Putting It into Practice

IT IMPROVES YOUR EFFICIENCY AND
EFFECTIVENESS AS A LEADER.

By taking a conscious approach on how you are doing things as a leader, you are actually creating a healthy work environment.

The complete description of acceptable and unacceptable behaviors can be found on the Treasury Board Secretariat web page of Canada.ca.

The KLC provide a roadmap for assessing leadership effectiveness based on behaviours from supervisors up to the deputy minister (president) of the organization.

In order to do your own self-assessment, take the behaviors and write up some examples of how you are demonstrating this competency. It is not just good enough to say that I do this, but if someone does not know this, how can they see it? How do you know this to be true? It would be great if you also have colleagues, employees, or supervisors that can confirm your examples. If it is not easy to find examples, then start to find ways to demonstrate this competency in your existing role.

Examples:

Create Vision and Strategy

- Use of a project plan or strengths, weaknesses, opportunities, and threats (SWOT) analysis to engage employees, clients, and partners.

- Make a vision board to share with your family for the goals for the year.

Mobilize People

- Engage your colleagues in a conversation on how to improve your work.
- Coordinate a bottle drive for a local charity.

Uphold Integrity and Respect

- Respect the privacy of clients by making sure no one can hear what they are sharing with you.
- Seek friends with a different perspective than yours.

Collaborate with Partners and Stakeholders

- Ask for the perspective of experts in the domain. Example: Ask experts in human resources when dealing with challenging situations at work.
- Find businesses to sponsor sporting events.

Promote Innovation and Change

- Ask yourself how you could do things differently, and do it!
- Find something new to do with your family.

Achieve Results

- Keep track of your own productivity and the quality of services you are providing.
- Look at where you are spending your time at home. Does it support your happiness or not?

I also used these as I was preparing myself for competitive processes. I made sure I was able to speak to each dimension while using some examples. The following is an example of my own experience. I will use integrity and respect, since this is the one that seems to be the hardest to find an example:

Definition: Leaders exemplify ethical practices, professionalism and personal integrity. They create respectful and trusting work environments where sound advice is valued. They encourage the expression of diverse opinions and perspectives, while fostering collegiality. Leaders are self-aware and seek out opportunities for personal growth.

Examples of effective behaviours at the Director General level. ("Key Leadership Competency Profile and Examples of Effective and Ineffective Behaviours," Canada.ca)

All my career, I have led teams in rural areas or in small town/ cities in Canada. I had to assess the impacts of my behavior professionally and personally in my community. This is especially true when the Federal Public Service is the biggest employer in town.

When I managed the biggest investigation in my department's history, I had to be extra vigilant. It soon became apparent that there was going to be tension between the need for service and integrity of procedural fairness for the public interest.

There was a tragedy in a city that I lived that had multiple deaths and severe injuries. My department was responsible for conducting the investigation into the events. My team did the fact-finding, root cause analysis, and made a recommendation to the minister. Since I was responsible for making a recommendation, I took the role of project lead for this high-profile file.

I created a privacy wall between the employees performing the investigation by having a specific team dedicated to the task. I procured resources, such as an independent drive to store the information. Employees had their own locked room for debriefing. I reminded all staff of "the need to know" policy.

I chose the best health and safety officers (HSO) for the position: One senior investigator was solid in the health and safety field; and the other was equally qualified, a little bit more reserved, and spoke French. In each location, I also had two other HSOs supporting them in their work. I secured the services of Health Canada for the employees involved in this work. I ensured that they were properly debriefed on a regular basis.

As the team completed the work, I had regular updates with my director general (DG) and assistant deputy minister (ADM). Because of my experience in root cause analysis, I was a sounding board for my lead investigator. I added a third-party leadership perspective to the investigation.

Once the prosecution recommendation was sent to the Department of Justice, they became in charge of the file. I was able to strategically ensure a great collaboration with our lawyer. I had regular communication with him, as he needed my staff to assist. I was able to represent the interest of the department.

The process from beginning to end lasted approximately four years. I ensured the team members were seeing their Employee Assistance Program (EAP) counsellor on a regular basis. I also insisted that the officers take their vacation leave. We celebrated key milestones. It was important to recognize the excellent work performed even if we did not know the outcome of the investigation.

After the investigation, I led a lesson-learned exercise with the team, the leadership, and the stakeholders. This is where I identified the tensions at play in a major investigation. On one hand, it is important to arrive at a timely decision, considering all the stakeholders involved. On the other hand, the procedural fairness needs to be respected. Both these values are essential and need to be balanced. Therefore, it takes a strong team and leaders to handle these types of files.

The fact that I managed and controlled the communication was a critical success factor. The team was able to perform their work, and I was able to manage the inquiries. All the levels of the organization were interested in this file. I ensured that my DG and ADM's concerns were addressed and that the file was progressing as it should.

The results of the lessons learned in this file were also applied nationally within the department. It served as a model for large case management.

The verdict was in favor of the government. The impact of this decision is still felt in the industry today. The health and safety of their employees is forever changed. The families told me directly how appreciative they were of our work. The quality of the work was also recognized as we received an External Services Award of Excellence. The management of this file was the hardest and most fulfilling experience of my career.

As you can see, my actions in the workplace mattered for the employees, the clients, and the organization. For more example, I would encourage you to go on my website (notetoselflearningsolutions.ca) under "Key Leadership Competencies." You will get some examples of my experiences. They were in large part, what helped me to receive promotions with the respect of my employees and my peers.

As I matured throughout my career, I noticed that the use of the KLCs was more than just preparation; they were actually powerful and made a difference in my leadership style. If I am not getting the results I want, I go back to the competencies and do a check-in to see what I missed. I remember a time when I developed an excellent approach to resolve an issue. It was textbook perfect. The only thing that I forgot was to check-in with the people doing the work. Dah!

When I did a test, I found some critical errors in my design. I was able to change it just in time. It reminded me of the criticality of each competency. The KLCs are what I do, but *who* I am also has big impacts.

Does It Make a Difference in Who I Am?

CHARACTER-BASED LEADERSHIP—WHO AM I?

In my leadership role, I have a tendency to be really innovative and have a focus on people. This is most likely a result of my experience and education. At the same time, I need to remind myself on a regular basis that I have a service to deliver. I need to show results for my accountabilities. It is OK for me to do great stuff, but if my big rocks are not taken care of, I will have issues at work.

The KLCs are a leading indicator for me to excel. Just doing the work is no longer good enough; I need to be authentic and believe in what I am doing. Now the public service is keeping their leaders at higher standards by looking at their character.

As mentioned, not *only what* you do will matter, but also *who* you are. The character-based leadership model is being adopted in several departments to reinforce the public service values:

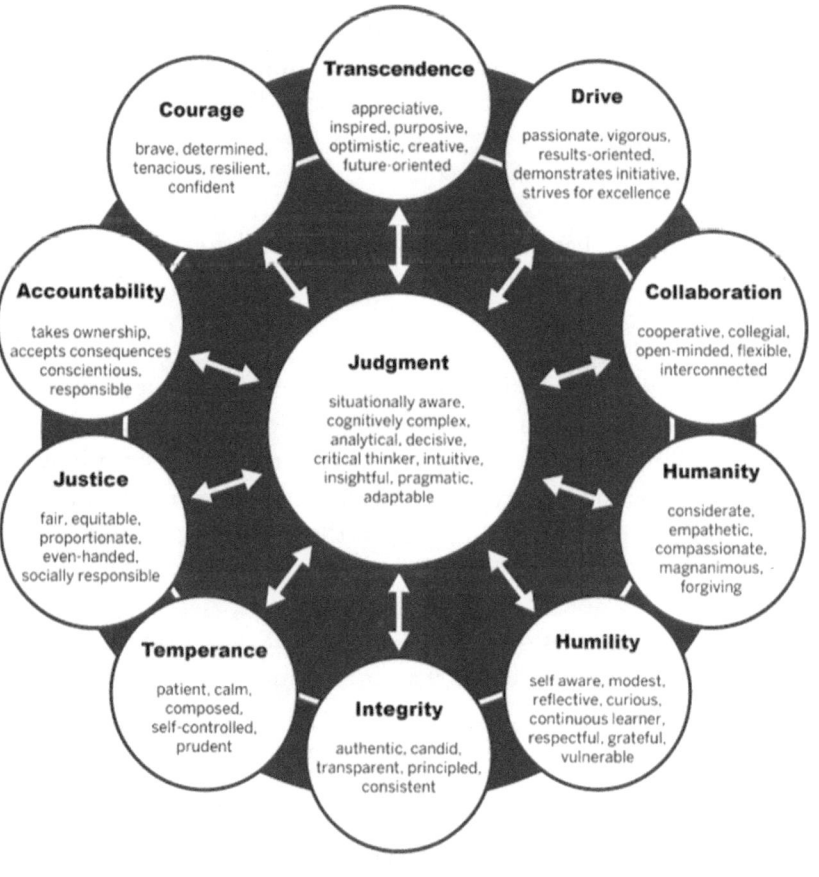

In summary, our behaviors are influenced by our biases. Any type of biases affects our judgement, especially as leaders. It will trigger the dimensions of our character that impact our leadership effectiveness. For example, if I think someone is not being fair, my sense of justice might become excessive, and I will not want to collaborate with some people because of that. This could yield negative business results, as all our work is interconnected.

I will provide you with another example of strengths that could become weaknesses.

A manager brought to my attention that the clocks in my office showed different times. In a building of six floors, every conference or training room would have differences of five to fifteen minutes.

Over the years, our finance and administration group would go periodically to change the batteries and put the clocks all at the same time. This lasted only for a couple of days, and then it would go back to lagging.

It encouraged interesting behaviors where employees would leave on a break with the time of one clock and would come back looking at another. Breaks would last over fifteen minutes depending on the clock you looked at. This situation happened in both offices that I was leading. I put this situation in the back of my head as a "to-do eventually."

After a few months, the situation surfaced twice in the same week. First, another leader was complaining about being late because of the clocks. Then a union representative told me that an employee was reprimanded because he was late because of the clocks.

This is where I said enough is enough. My drive kicked into overdrive, and I asked my responsible manager to take out all the clocks. He advised me against this. I called another manager to get his opinion (he was on my side). I instructed my manager to do it, and his objections were duly noted. Then I left for vacation.

Well, the next day the situation exploded. I was at the airport when my replacement called me to say that the unions and employees were all up in arms because the clocks were off the walls. I reminded them that we have cells and computers that provide more accurate time.

Once I came back from vacation, I dealt appropriately with the downfalls of this situation by apologizing for not taking the time to consult and do things right. My impatience supported my ability to get things done. At the same time, it went against every change management practices. This imbalance affected my judgment. I did have to say I am sorry about the way things were handled and adjusted the strategy by taking a step back. By the way, the only concession I made was to have clocks in training rooms.

The above reflection allowed me to be real and vulnerable to my organization; it facilitated my gaining of credibility and trust with my employees.

One key element of success in exploring character leadership is to understand our preferences with acceptance. There are some self-assessment tools to explore one's communication styles, emotional intelligence, and strengths on the leadership traits wheel. These provide a picture of our favorite practices. The assessments helped to identify some of my blind spots when it came to excess or deficiency in a dimension. The workplace strategies for mental health website provides some assessments that you can explore: "Assessments, Tools and Workshops" (workplacestrategiesformentalhealth.com).

Now What?

In order to dive deeper into our experiences, learning circles bring a practical lens and reinforce some of our leadership practices. Leadership becomes a conscious effort by taking every opportunity to question the work that we do. As such, coming from a place of strength and understanding.

For example, one of my leaders felt that he had no control over the upcoming decisions. Even if he was explicitly told, "This is your department and [you] take the decisions. Make sure you document your rationale and engage the right people." He did not want to ruffle any feathers because he was a people person. In a conflictual situation, he did not have the courage to confront the situation. Having the courage is to be open to the vulnerability that there can be another version that you are not aware of and have the confidence to question the other person without fear of reprisal.

This character-based leadership me reinforce that there are no right or wrong ways to lead. There are some effective and efficient ways, depending on the situation and employees involved.

The character-based leadership and the key leadership competencies are practices in one's toolkit. When I am not getting the results, I (again) reflect on my past practices. Are they bringing me closer to my intended results? If not, ask why, why, why. A trusted friend or colleague can also provide me with this external perspective. Especially when I have strong emotions or opinions about something, I take a moment to check with someone that I know will give me an honest answer. It might not be what I want to hear, but then I have information to move forward.

At the end of the day, I do not want to be right; I want to do the right thing. Looking at my competencies or dimensions of my character does not make me good or bad. It provides me with some intelligence on what are some practices that I am favoring. To get different results, I need to do different things, and this is where the other competencies and dimensions of the character become handy to develop.

Do I Dare to Ask?

WHY DOES ALL THIS MATTER ANYWAY?

Over the years in my leadership role, I stayed close to these competencies. It was a way for me to audit my growth and my areas of development. In my first leadership role, I found that there was no road map to being a formal leader. My experience helped me develop myself in line with these. This is a major reason why I am writing this book. I wanted to share with you these learnings so they become part of your toolkit.

Today I provide feedback to my direct reports using the CBL wheel. It serves to depersonalize the experience and provide the leaders with some means of action for the future. The importance to attend to one's leadership style cannot be overstated.

In one of my past courses, I always remembered this phrase: "Every time you speak, you audition for leadership!" My call for leaders is to reflect on that quote (see picture). I added the part of being kind, because at the end of the day, in the present moment, we are all authors of our own words.

No matter what we say verbally or with our non-verbal cues, employees will interpret our behavior as we are carefully watched. Employees need to understand our cues in order to implement our directions.

I think it might be the great poet Rumi that said, "Before you speak, let your words pass through these three gates: Is it true? Is it necessary? Is it kind?" This practice is valid no matter what your role is in the organization. Even if you are not in a formal leadership position, just by being in the position you are in, in your work, you are influencing someone's experience (client, colleague, or supervisor). It is up you to choose your words wisely, as we are authors of our words; please make it kind.

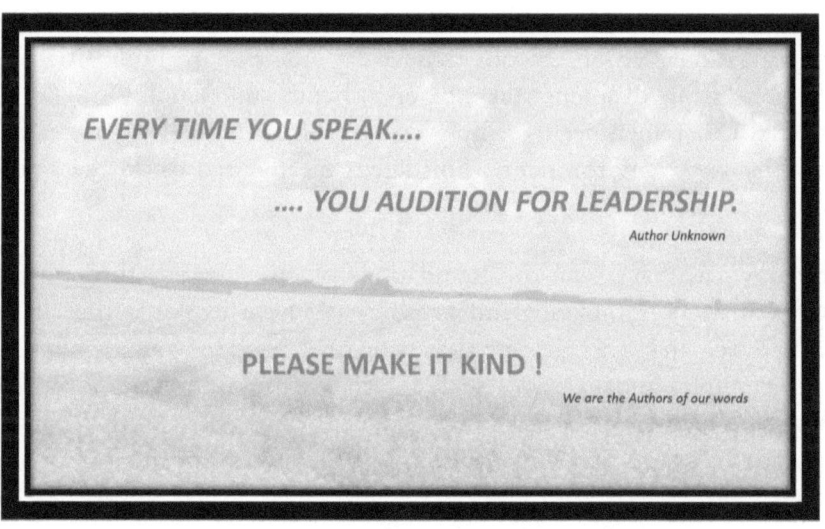

EVERY TIME YOU SPEAK....

.... YOU AUDITION FOR LEADERSHIP.

Author Unknown

PLEASE MAKE IT KIND !

We are the Authors of our words

Finally, in my humble opinion, being a leader needs to be a conscious decision. It is not an easy role at all, and it has a bunch of accountabilities. It is not for the faint of heart. The consequences of doing an average job can have negative impacts, such as creating a space for doubt, lack of trust, missed opportunities, etc. I have seen this so many times—leaders being afraid to make the hard decisions because of all valid reasons. They were not looking at the reason of why to do it; they were looking at preserving the status quo.

In the enclosed graphic, the center shows that we all have goals, expectations, visions, or missions. I found that my perception was influenced positively or negatively by my interpretation of my environment. If my experience brought me closer to my expectations, I

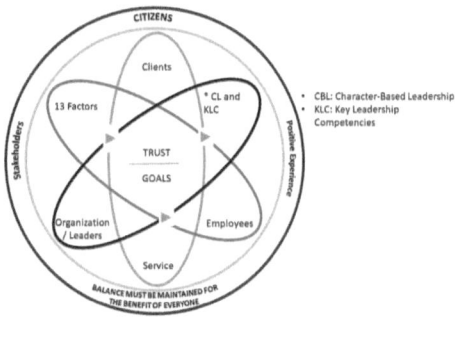

was open to trust. If not, then I felt threatened, and I closed myself. This is why I find it extremely important to understand what motivates me and my staff.

Why are they getting up in the morning? I feel it essential to understand my direct reports and personal goals, linking it to the organizational vision. In our day-to-day life, we are bombarded by requests from different stakeholders, clients, and employees. I find strength in remembering why I do what I do (which is to create a healthy work environment). This keeps me focused to do the heavy lifting.

By now, we have seen the foundations of my thinking through the work matters framework and graphic. We have explored the client, employee, and organizational perspective. I hope you appreciated the examples and exercises so far. Now, how can we bring all this together? What are the risks and what can we do about this? What are the consequences of doing nothing? Why should you care?

I would like to say thank you to the Treasury Board Secretariat for providing this direction with the MAF and KLCs; they shaped my leadership style. I also want to say thank you to the Ivey League for their continued interest in looking at character as part of leadership. This is unchartered territory that opens the conversation of humility and transcendence in the workplace. It changes the conversation from what I manage, to who I am and how I am transformed through my leadership practices.

"*Note to Self*"
Learning Solutions

_____

_____

_____

_____

_____

_____

_____

_____

_____

BRINGING IT ALL TOGETHER

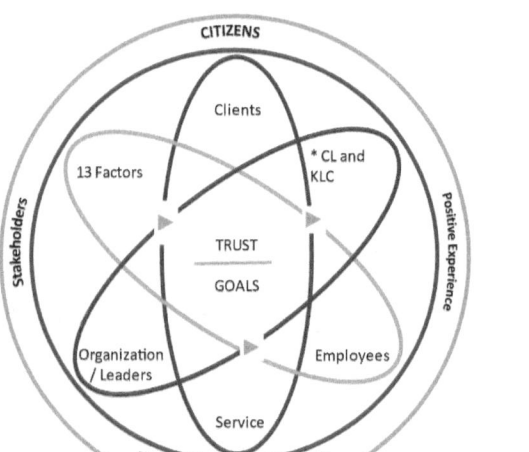

A Recap, Anyone?

PLEASE DO, NATHALIE.

At the beginning, I mentioned that this book will help you see the organization holistically. Let's have a quick look to see where we are at. This graph represents a summary of our key learnings.

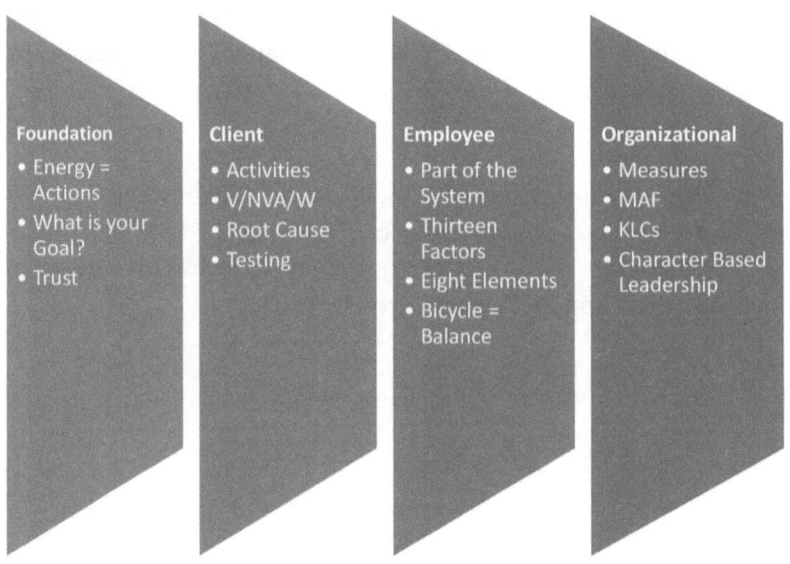

Foundation
- Energy = Actions
- What is your Goal?
- Trust

Client
- Activities
- V/NVA/W
- Root Cause
- Testing

Employee
- Part of the System
- Thirteen Factors
- Eight Elements
- Bicycle = Balance

Organizational
- Measures
- MAF
- KLCs
- Character Based Leadership

We have learned that our actions are influenced by our goals and our perception of trust. Do we trust that we will achieve our objectives? We have seen some details on how the three perspectives (client, employee, and organizational) in a business affect the outcome and results. Hopefully, by now, you will agree that all three perspectives are valuable to you. If not, let's chat.

I provided great examples of how these concepts can be applied to any project, program delivery, or service. Questioning yourself in everything you do: What are the activities you choose to adopt? Are they adding value? Are they necessary but stopping the flow (NVA)? Or are they not necessary at all and are actually considered waste? And most importantly, why are they occurring in the first place?

Are you and other employees bringing the best version of yourselves to work? If not, what are some of the conditions missing or needing improvement? Do you need to manage your workload differently? Do you need to improve your work conditions? Are you taking care of yourself? Which elements are your strengths, and what do you need to pay attention to? Is your bicycle (see analogy on page 41) going straight on the road or straight into a ditch?

We also learned that what gets measured gets done. The management accountability framework provides interesting components to explore our management effectiveness. The key leadership competencies and the character leadership dimensions are also essential to analyse the quality of our actions.

This has been our journey so far, now what? Where do we go from here? This journey is continuously evolving. In the role of a learner, there is only a wide-open road ahead. Let's look at this adventure from an organizational and individual perspective.

Are We Looking at the Big Picture?

ORGANIZATIONAL LEARNING VIEW

Please remember that learning is a lifelong journey. I am still travelling this path. I would like to share with you what caught my attention so far.

Over the years, I have heard that organizations are risk adverse, and we need to take intelligent risks—what does this mean? For me, it is synonymous with continuous organizational learning. The big question is, How does an organization learn? My answer: Through its clients and employees (teams). The caveat is that it needs to be done with intention.

We are good at identifying issues, and great strategies and implementation are somewhat interesting to witness. Any great idea, work process improvement, or simply a change, no matter how big or small, needs to be implemented systematically to be able to learn the risks, concerns, bottlenecks, etc.

In the previous chapters, I mentioned process improvement. I will now go deeper into understanding of what is behind the concepts and implementation. This view will be exploring three elements: One, the way we implement things (validation and implementation); two, the way we continuously improve the organization; and three, the way we involve people in change.

Let's Just Do the Thing

VALIDATION AND IMPLEMENTATION PROCESS (VIP).

Early in my career, I observed that we were great at generating ideas but not so much at implementation. We wanted results now and fast. When I became aware of process management, I felt the need to develop another course, which was an approach to validate assumptions and implement solutions. A very important process (VIP) to be done consciously. In reality, VIP stands for validation and implementation process (see picture).

Validation and Implementation Process (VIP)

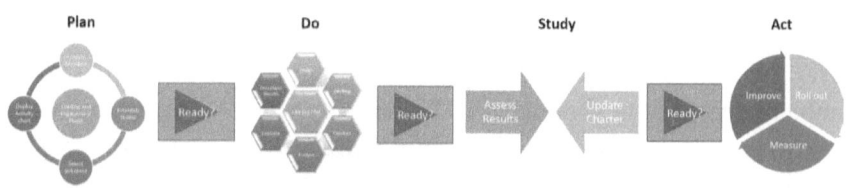

In my humble opinion, any learning effort needs to go through this gate: plan-do-study-act model. This is in reference to Dr. Deming, the grandfather of total quality management (TQM). Today, I prefer the lead-plan-do-study-act because by leading, you are telling the story as well.

There is a full methodology behind each step that I would be happy to discuss. For now, I will provide a brief description of each section.

This work was influenced by two great thinkers: Dr. Michael Hammer and Dr. Joseph Juran. These two authors influenced the development and application of this approach. You will also notice that these steps are familiar if you have experience leading technology projects.

Leading Engagement and Planning Phase

Let's start from the beginning. The planning phase of this process can be viewed in summary by engaging the leadership to provide the resources and setting the boundaries for the project.

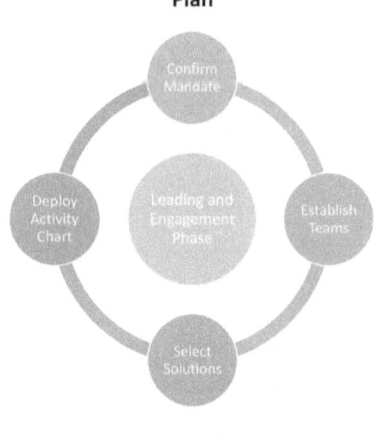

Please do not skip any steps, even if you think it is clear, it will come back to haunt you. It did for me.

There is a strategic reason behind each step; hence, leaders need to be actively engaged. Confirming mandate is to ensure that there is a common understanding on the reasoning behind the implementation.

In establishing the team, you might want to ensure that you have subject matter experts as well as new employees. New employees will bring an external perspective.

Selecting solutions is to ensure that the team understands what is under study. If there was a time delay between the proposed ideas and implementation, there might be a need to question the validity of the solutions. Sometimes, there will be a requirement to go back and design solutions to better fit the business needs.

Please make sure that the new solutions are optimizing the value, minimizing the non-value work, and eliminating waste (see chapters on client perspective for more details).

Deploying the activity chart is to frame your work in a chart to gain a consensus on the deployment of the project. The above steps are good sound project management practices. Be careful not to get caught into the details and going too deep in charting your course. The purpose of this phase is to set boundaries for the project. It serves as terms of references for the work to be accomplished in the next phases.

Do Phase

In this phase, you will test your product or your process. Is it achieving what you intended? This is the time to make errors and learn from them. It is the time to test all assumptions and see what you have come up. It is what I call learning by design. In the lab, you will test your hypothesis in a safe environment, while during the pilot you will engage clients of the processes or products.

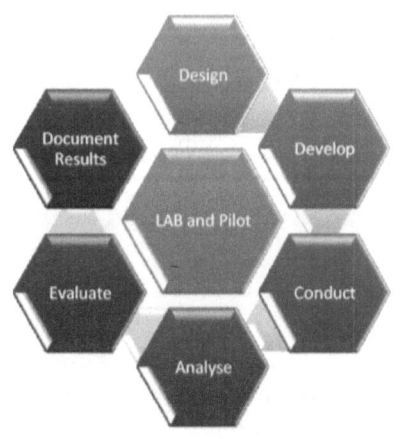

As you can see, the steps are basically the same. This approach finds its source in *Juran's Quality Handbook* (chapter 47) and Dr. Michael Hammer's (2002) theory of life in a lab/pilot. In a pilot, you will test the activities that performing in the lab does not. In real terms, this refers to client processes.

The other distinction from traditional testing is that you will also test your communication, training, and measurement products. It is a mini proof of concepts that you will be doing.

Why is it so important not to skip steps? Because you will learn different things at each stage. This is what we call intelligent risk taking or learning organization.

In my career, I have experienced the benefits of this approach several times. One time, an idea came up to implement a new form for our clients. We first agreed that we would test it before going out to all clients (thousands of them). We tested the form with employees working in the field (this was our lab).

In a nutshell, we identified all the requirements and, especially, our goals and measures of success. We tested it with other parts of our operations to make sure it made sense. We included in our testing the communication products and detailed instructions that we planned to send to clients. We did a great job stabilizing the lab.

We learned a great deal. The biggest one is that we cannot implement a form without reviewing the existing process. Once our results were stable, we moved to the next step.

But wait, there was a change in government, and there was an incident that paused our work for approximately six months. Before we started again, we reviewed our information to ensure that the conditions were similar to where we left off. Then we formed a team and continued our work.

In the pilot phase, we chose some of our clients that we had great relationships and that were different in size. We started the activities with our communication products, had information sessions, provided clients with contact employees, and trained them on the new process that the form required.

As we tested with clients, we soon realized that the client's application of processes was not the same as the governments. They gave access to their system where the work was being performed (by hundreds of leaders). On the other hand, the authorized authority to access the employer's business account was only a select few in the business. If we continued in that direction, our mandate would not be achieved and the cost of administrating this new process (form) would outweigh the benefits.

After a few months in the process, the analysis of the results clearly showed that going forward would not benefit the clients, the employees, nor the program. We documented our experience, thanked our clients for their contributions, and found another way to achieve our results.

Please note that the lab and pilot phase of a project could also be done in support of automated tools, such as BPMN. BPMN stands for business process modeling notation—a standard set of mapping symbols that enables accurate process simulation. BPMN simulations can provide information you need to compile, most notably:

- Cycle and process times
- Resource requirements, including employee requirements

Now that you have data for your project, how are you managing the project?

Still Doing the Thing?

VALIDATION AND IMPLEMENTATION
PROCESS (VIP), LET'S CONTINUE.

In order to address changes in the environment, I designed some gates in the validation and implementation process.

Study and Act Phases

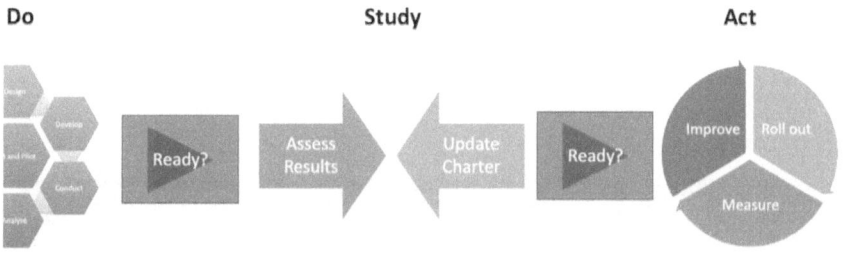

The three decision points being "Ready?" are to address the instability of a work environment. Only when your critical success factors are met should you stop testing.

The other gate is to move forward, and this can take some time, which leads us into assessing results component. This is a reflection time before you go into full implementation (roll out) to make sure that you really want to do this.

The last part of this process is the roll out to other parts of the organization. I would also recommend doing it in a phased approach so that you can still learn. I have yet to meet an organization that is not special or have different considerations. By using a phased approach (especially if there is technology involved), it assures that you are continuously learning.

The implementation strategy (roll out) will depend on your operational reality. Are there lots of changes going on right now? If yes, be strategic in your phases. You need to show results every three to six months. A full project should be done in eighteen to twenty-four months. Longer than this, there is a chance that people will lose interest and that the environment will change too much or that the issue you are trying to fix will be irrelevant.

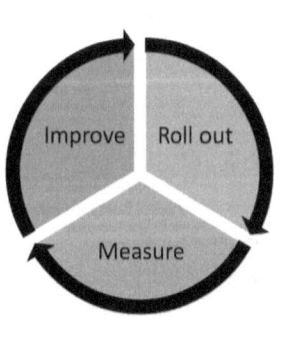

Let's have an example. Implement a new way of working. I could divide the implementation of in three phases:

1. Develop and test internal and external communications products
2. Develop and test processes and procedures on new ways of working
3. Train employees

Activities	2022				2023			
	Jan-March	April-June	July-Sept	Oct-Dec	Jan-March	April-June	July-Sept	Oct-Dec
Test Internal Communication Products	L,P	R						
Develop and test new process		L	P	R				
Develop and test procedures		L	P	R				
Train Employees			L	P,R				
Test External Coms			L	P	R			
Report results				L	P, R			
Cumulative months	3	6	9	12	15	18	21	24

L: Laboratory

P: Pilot

R: Roll-out

You will notice that there are parallel activities and some phases (L, P, R) can be done at the same time. I use quarters to reflect the strategies, but weeks and days can also be used. It would be important to give some time to analyse the experience, adapt the products, and share the results.

I mentioned the measurement system in the last chapter. These ensure that we are continuously improving the results for our clients. They also need to be designed and tested. The measurement topic was discussed in lengths (see page 58), and continuous process improvement is the next topic to review.

You can apply the VIP approach to anything you do, and it does not take time. For example, if you want to write an important email to someone. First, you do your write-up (lab). You might want to think about the wording, the risks of sending the email, and the consequences. Once satisfied, you let a friend read it (pilot). After modifying the email, you then send it or not. If it is too risky to do it by email, then you choose an in-person conversation and repeat the process.

The Thing Is Done, Now What?

Continuous process improvement (CPI)—I chose the perspective of continuous process improvement because it has the means to continually question your activities and build on your lessons learned. This, for me, is excellence in everything we do.

Dr. Michael Hammer influenced my perspective when it comes to continuous improvement. The process life cycle (2002) operationalizes improvements and brings everything together. Not every process should be reengineered, and likewise, not every process should be incrementally improved. Furthermore, some of them we should just not touch, because it is a question of execution and training, not a systemic issue!

Graphic: Continuous improvement process

If you look at this model, it is closely related to Dr. E. Deming's plan-do-study-act and Dr. Hammer's teachings. As I look at these models, although the references are dated (2002), the essence of the theory proven, in my opinion, is still valid. I observed the work of consultants within the public service that were implementing these strategies in 2022. I will now go deeper in intentionally improving the organization.

In my work experience, we usually measure the outputs of our work. This does not favor our employees. They are much more involved in actually doing the work and it starts with establishing expectations that link to clients' needs.

Over the years, I found it useful to have a systematic approach to analyse data. I revert to process improvement concepts, such as LEAN and methods proposed in chapter client perspective. As we perform our work, I like it to be deliberate. The data on our work processes, results from our clients, our tools, training, and communication products provides me with some insights on potential improvements.

Determining the solutions needs to look also at the root causes why something is happening. One needs to ensure that in the analysis the underlying factors are covered. Too often, I witnessed that we looked at trends and inferred causality without data to support it.

Furthermore, in determining the solutions a decision point needs to be answered. Is the gap due to a question of execution? Does this mean the employee received all the tools, training, coaching, etc. to perform the work? If yes, then it is most likely a systemic issue. Once, the analysis shows that it is systemic, the gravity will determine if it is an incremental improvement or a full-blown redesign. This step is very important; you do not want to improve something that should not be done at all. One rule of thumb could be that if the data suggests an impact on business outcomes, it was an issue for many years, and all the efforts did not yield intended results, then it could lead to a redesign.

Finally, the process needs to be visible. Even if we have standard operating procedures, the process, in which they perform, needs to be clear. It does not matter if it is an incremental improvement or a full-blown redesign or even just implementing a new way of doing business. In mapping the process, it is a great way to communicate the work expectations.

All this work needs to be aligned with the organizational objectives. I have to say, that the way I led organizations in the past was with this mindset. I am still learning the conditions to make it real. I wanted to provide you with a framework; now, it is up to you to go deeper. Let's share our insights at notetoselflearnigsolutions.ca.

We have reviewed the technical process side of continuous improvement. Now let's have a glimpse at the people side.

People Again?

INVOLVING PEOPLE IN THE BUSINESS.

As you saw in the above approach, to implement an improvement in an organization starts and ends with people (either employees or clients).

Sometimes, it is too risky to involve clients in the testing phases of change. I would encourage you to get their voice through surveys or other types of data (e.g., quality) that provide the experience of the client. In a pilot, it will be the perfect opportunity to validate your hypothesis in a safe environment.

In the information that was provided this far, you saw that we are inclusive with employees. They need to be part of the designing of the solutions, the implementation, and improvement phases. Furthermore, we saw the criticality of the role of employees in the workplace, for example, in participating in workplace committees and bringing their expertise on client issues.

Depending on the individual, you might want to include them at different parts of the process. For a highly creative person, the design of the solutions or exploring root causes is a great place. Employees that are detail-oriented would show their strengths in the validation and implementation phases where they can test their assumptions.

The literature on change management is quite extensive. Prosci's approach has helped me over the years. The activities can be grouped in four categories: (1) communication, (2) training and development, (3) dealing with reaction to changes, and (4) celebrating/reinforcing appropriate behaviors.

My experience showed if I had activities in these four areas, the success of my project was more likely. As I read these words, I cannot find anything that was not a success. There where lessons learned and adjustments for sure, but because I had a systematic approach to testing and implementing activities, it was positive. Actually, there is one time it was not a success; it was because I went off-script (see the story about the clocks).

I would like to expand on these four areas a bit by providing some key points:

Communication: Please ensure that you have a two-way communication strategy. You can be really sophisticated when it comes to communication, as it is a discipline in itself. In my experience, communication is always a factor that needs to be addressed, it adds to the complexity of an issue.

In order to guide my efforts, I used an adult education perspective by making information easy to understand and fun. I love creating a work environment where we exchange and build on each other's perspective. No matter what your project, your communication strategy will need to be planned at the beginning.

Training and Development: Over the years, I learned not to assume that people are understanding everything that is implemented. We are working from a set of assumptions that formulate our way of thinking. My priority is not yours. Even if it is just to check our understanding, we need to make sure that we increase our chances of us implementing something with similar results by offering some training. Again, training and development is a discipline in itself. In order to get me out of trouble, the principles of adult education such as Lunsford (2018) video on the seven characteristics of adult learners was an inspiration for me to set the stage to facilitate training and learning. My invitation to learn is transformative and

- interactive,
- meaningful,
- all about the learner,
- practical,
- flexible,

- relatable, and
- personalized.

Yes, I need to be a little more creative to develop the products that respect these guidelines; but in my humble experience, it is worth it. People will retain more information because they are living an experience. I cannot count the number of emails and personal messages from participants on the effectiveness of my approaches.

Dealing with Reaction to Change: If you notice, I did not say resistance to change. We all experience change differently. I love change at work. I found innovative ways to do my work on a regular basis; I love to learn and experiment. But at a restaurant, I mostly eat the same thing and go to the same restaurant. I know exactly what I want and the experience I will get. Only occasionally will I change.

In the literature, you will find that people's reaction to change can be viewed on the bell curve. For illustration purposes: 5 percent of the people already made the change; 5 percent will never want to change (for various reasons, including retirement this year); and 90 percent will accept new roles and responsibilities with the appropriate tools, training, and understanding.

There is a wealth of resources to provide you guidance on change management strategies. These four themes are to keep you out of jail. You need to adapt them to the context you are dealing with. It will help you plan ahead and manage the reaction to change. A reaction is unavoidable; the opportunity is to put the chances on your side to make it a positive experience. Clear communication, appropriate training, and reward appropriate behaviors are all actions we control to make the change successful.

Reinforcing Appropriate Behaviors: This theme should not come as a surprise. We saw that what gets measured gets done and that positive experiences, over time, influence the trust we have in a person. These are examples of reinforcing the appropriate behavior.

In any changes, we need to be careful on the messages and actions, verbal and non-verbal. At the same time, it is something that we might forget if we do not consciously identify our critical success factors. The challenge is to be explicit and communicate early our successes and lessons learned. I know, sometimes, I am too busy with the implementation that I forget to tell the story. I learned to make the effort and dedicate resources to pay attention to this important component. Again, I need to emphasize that every time we speak, we audition for leadership. What we focus on will give employees the indicators of what matters to us.

All the above processes, such as validation and implementation process, change management, continuous learning through continuous process improvement support, and measuring the right things are all part of a learning organization to support reinforcing the appropriate behaviors.

Now what? If you are a formal leader, continuously work on your competencies because they influence your mindset, which, in turn, influences the decisions you make, the approaches you choose, and the actions you take.

So far, I have been talking about bringing everything together at the organizational level. In my opinion, in order to sustain the changes over time, it needs to also be connected to the individual learning perspective.

What about MOI?

INDIVIDUAL LEARNING VIEW.

In each of the chapters, you were invited to integrate your learnings either by reflection or by practical exercises. As adult learners, we need to practice what we learn in order to fully appreciate our experiences and grow from them. There are no easy solutions here; I gave you lots of theories, examples, and compelling reasons why the concepts and approaches in this book yield results. Now it is up to you!

What are the consequences of not taking care of each perspective in the framework? What are the consequences of doing nothing?

1. **Clients:** It affects the confidence in government or in your brand. Clients might not buy what you are selling.
2. **Employees:** It affects the confidence in senior management, which includes team leaders. Employees might not believe you.
3. **Leaders:** It affects trust in themselves and the organization's trust in them to deliver. Your boss might micromanage you. You might be resistant to making timely decisions.

Confidence equals trust, which can be expressed by having positive experiences over time. I heard my colleagues reflecting why employees do not have confidence in leadership; could it be that we are not attending to the right things?

You could write a whole chapter just on this truth (and maybe that is still to come?). What does it look like for leaders to intentionally invite employees into the role of co-creating a positive work environment? What is the impact on client service when this happens well? What could you draw from your wealth of experience?

As you can see, all your actions have consequences. No matter what we do or say, it will create a synergy that will affect people, no matter if you are in a leadership position or not. Your interactions with your clients can have a positive or negative impact.

Our role as leaders, regardless of level, is to create consistent positive experiences for the benefit of the three stakeholders; at the same time, maintaining balance amongst the three is the key to success. Over time, our deliberate actions will link back to service excellence for the benefit of  all our clients and citizens. This will demonstrate commitment and consistency, as well as a capability to sustain efforts to create and maintain a healthy work environment.

For this to occur, I found it beneficial to have a mind that is curious. I have the courage to be confident and know that I am safe. No one can hurt me when I bring the best version of myself to work. Will they try? For sure. Will they succeed? No! In my experience, no one can touch what is authentic and real. Sure, I get disappointed and angry with people, but they cannot reach me in my core. I am safe, and it is my belief that you can be too.

In order to be in that space, one also needs a growth mindset. This is, basically, knowing that you will make choices; and whatever choices you make, you will get some benefits and some challenges. The idea is to learn from setbacks and challenges to increase your skills and tools in your toolbox. Lancaster (2020) views mistakes like the doorway to success. They can be harnessed to support growth and development. Once we are comfortable with our own imperfections, then the world is accessible to us. We will create the conditions to learn from our daily reality, no matter if it is good or bad.

As we translate this level of comfort with ourselves into the business, we will take some intelligent risks. We will create the conditions to manage the vulnerabilities of our systems, processes, etc. We will lead from a place of strength and authenticity. This is my wish for you.

From the Heart:

Now I need to say that to be human at work is conscious work. I remind myself of my qualities on a regular basis. Presently, I need to remind myself to have the courage to speak in big groups. Just like everyone, I fear making a fool of myself. I started a new job, and I am in a learning mode. Because of my background, people sometime refer to me as the expert. Well, this puts additional pressure on me because I do not consider myself an expert. There is way too much to learn. This additional pressure to have the right answers is something I am working on.

When I feel the pressure, I listen to it by being in the present moment. I open myself to a message; basically, does it feel right to intervene? I wait for the answer by reflecting on how I see things. Then I release all outcomes and speak from the heart. I learned this LORRAX technique from Sky Nelson-Isaacs book *Living in the Flow* (2019).

If the result is a brilliant intervention, I am proud of myself. If I make an error, I listen and learn. I am learning that perfection does not exist, and I need to be perfect in my imperfection. People will always judge me from the colour of their own lenses. The people that embrace life as a learning journey are by my side, creating healthy work environments where employees can bring the best version of themselves to work.

At the end of the day, never give up continuing to learn as you navigate through your journey. Every time you learn something new, it builds on your experience and makes you stronger. Being real is not something outside of yourself; it is part of who you are.

As you grow, your skillset is growing even stronger because of your authenticity—this is where you are safe. Mooji's words eloquently summarize my thoughts: "It takes a lot of energy to be a person. It takes no energy to be yourself."

> *Thank you to Dr. Joseph Duran, Dr. Deming, and all of you that contributed to the Total Quality Management discipline over the years. As you can see, it did influence me. Prosci also has been a critical influence. I purchased the books in their first version in 2002, and twenty years after, in 2022, I participated in another training session; and the information is relevant and still brings successful changes.*

Are You Done Yet?

NOPE . . . ANOTHER FEW THINGS . . .

This book is a labor of love. It is a thank you to the Canadian Public Service to share my last thirty years of work. I learned a great deal and I am continuing to learn. I started by saying that I am a fourth generation public servant. Most likely, it will end with me, but the service to Canada is forever embedded in our DNA.

As I see the future, I am embarking on another mandate for the federal public service. Again, I am thankful because I will get to work at the system level. I am excited about this. As this will most likely be my last mandate in the public service, I am facing it with peace, joy, and happiness, as I know I got this.

The last thirty years have brought me to where I am today. A big thank you to all of you I met on this journey. You know who you are. You have shaped me to be the woman and leader that I am today.

It took me lots of courage to write this book; I am not even sure if anyone will learn something from my experience. The strength I get is through reading books. When I get scared, usually there is a book that appears. As I was writing, *The Everyday Hero Manifesto* appeared and gave me courage. Thank you, Robin Sharma, for your excellence and for helping me through this adventure.

I am happy 92 percent of the time because of you beautiful people that influenced my growth. Maybe there will be a time where I will tell the full story (the 8 percent). In the meantime, keep being perfect in your imperfection, as this is where excellence lies. I have been changed a lot by challenges over the year; now, I focus on the love. I am saying yes to the next chapter of my life.

My wish for you is to take the parts of this book that inspire you and go deeper. You have all the components to succeed in everything you do, to build on your experience and your expertise with this framework. As you saw, there are great resources at your disposal to start or continue your learning journey. I invite you all to be authentic, and in the words of Dewitt Jones, "Celebrate what is right with the world."

A big thank you to all of you who took the time and read this book. With gratitude, Nathalie White.

"Note to Self"
Learning Solutions

_____

_____

_____

_____

_____

_____

_____

_____

Smart People Helped Me throughout My Journey

THESE ARE MY REFERENCES:

Author Unknown. n.d. "Evidence-Based Actions for Psychological Competencies and Demands." Workplace Strategies for Mental Health. Retrieved January 17, 2022. https://www. workplacestrategiesformentalhealth.com/resources/evidence-based-actions-for-psychological-competencies-and-demands.

Author Unknown. n.d. "Facilitation Guide: Putting Growth and Awareness on the Agenda." Workplace Strategies for Mental Health. Retrieved January 17, 2022. https://wsmh-cms.mediresource.com/wsmh/assets/ncoudv400pc808k0.

Author Unknown. n.d. "Suggested Actions and Resources." Guarding Minds at Work. Retrieved January 17, 2022. https://www. guardingmindsatwork.ca/assets/pdfs/suggested-actions-resources.pdf.

Author Unknown. 2017. "Mental Health Continuum." Mental Health Commission. Retrieved January 18, 2022. https://theworkingmind.ca/sites/default/files/resources/r2mr_poster_en.pdf.

Byrne, Rhonda. 2021. *The Secret to Love, Health, and Money. A Masterclass.* New York, NY: *ATRIA Paperback.* February 2021.

Cohn, Sorin. 2015. *Innovation Metrics: Measuring Innovation for Tangible Performance.* Conference Board of Canada Webinar. July 22, 2015. 15:17 minutes.

Covey, Stephen M. R. 2016. *The Speed of Trust*. @LEAD. Presented by HR.com. Retrieved October 26, 2020. April 18, 2016. https://www.youtube.com/watch?v=lvIEfNyZ8B0.

CSA Group. n.d. "Psychological Health and Safety in the Workplace." Retrieved January 15, 2022. https://store.csagroup.org/ccrz__CCPage?pagekey=content&contentkey=Z1003HealthandSaftey_EN, https://www.csagroup.org/documents/codes-and-standards/publications/CAN_CSA-Z1003-13_BNQ_9700-803_2013_EN.pdf.

Demartini, John. 2021. Awakening with Spirit Summit 2021. August 31, 2021. theshiftnetwork.com.

Employment and Social Development Canada (ESDC). n.d. "Employer and Employee Duties." Retrieved January 15, 2022. https://www.canada.ca/en/employment-social-development/services/health-safety/reports/duties.html.

Government of Canada. n.d. "Key Leadership Competency Profile and Examples of Effective and Ineffective Behaviors." Retrieved July 22, 2022. https://www.canada.ca/en/treasury-board-secretariat/services/professional-development/key-leadership-competency-profile/examples-effective-ineffective-behaviours.html.

Government of Canada. n.d. "Management Accountability Framework." Retrieved July 22, 2022. https://www.canada.ca/en/treasury-board-secretariat/services/management-accountability-framework.html.

Hammer, Michael. 2002. Process Design and Implementation. Hammer and Company. January 22–25, 2002. Boston, Massachusetts, USA.

Institute for Citizen-Centred Service. n.d. "What Is Citizen-Centred Service?" Retrieved October 19, 2021. https://citizenfirst.ca/our-story/who-we-are/what-is-citizen-centred-service

Institute for Citizen-Centred Service. July 8, 2021. "Get the Highlights-Citizens First 2020." Retrieved October 27, 2021. https://citizenfirst.ca/newsroom.

Institute for Citizen-Centred Service. n.d. SVC Summary: Public Service Delivery Fundamentals. Retrieved January 22, 2022. https://citizenfirst.ca/our-work/learning-and-development/individual-modules/public-service-delivery-fundamentals.

Juran, Joseph M., and A. B Godfrey. (1998). *Juran's Quality Handbook.* 5th ed. McGraw Hill, USA.

Kélada, Joseph N. 2000. *Qualité totale: amelioration continue et réingénierie.* Québec, Canada: *Éditions Quafec.*

Lancaster, Andy. 2020. *Driving Performance Through Learning: Develop Employees through Effective Workplace Learning.* Kogan Page.

Lemay, Nathalie. 2009. "Applied Project." University of Waterloo, AB. January 20, 2009.

Lunsford, C. July 26, 2018. 7 *Characteristics of Adults Learners.* Retrieved February 6, 2021. https://www.youtube.com/watch?v=KeO5qaGFxaw.

Miller, Hannah L. 2022. "10 Ways of Building Trust as a Leader." Leaders Media. Retrieved July 22, 2022. https://leaders.com/articles/company-culture/building-trust/.

Nelson-Isaacs, Sky. 2019. *Living the Flow: the Science of Synchronicity and How Your Choices Shape your World.* Berkeley, California: North Atlantic Books

Russell, Nan S. June 30, 2012. "10 Behaviors that Demonstrate Trust." Psychology Today. Retrieved October 28, 2020. https://www.psychologytoday.com/us/blog/trust-the-new-workplace-currency/201206/10-behaviors-demonstrate-trust.

Swarbrick, Margaret. 2006. "A Wellness Approach." *Psychiatric Rehabilitation Journal* 29 (4): 311–314.

Treasury Board Secretariat (TBS). n.d. Values and Ethics Code for the Public Sector. Government of Canada. Retrieved January 15, 2022. https://www.tbs-sct.gc.ca/pol/doc-eng.aspx?id=25049.

Is This the End?

It is only the continuation of my journey . . . on to the next adventure . . . Stay tuned @notetoselflearningsolutions.ca.

Index

A

actions, 1
    deliberate, 8, 112
activities, 17–18
    value added, non-value added and
        waste, 22
atom, 1, 61

B

bicycle, 45–46, 94
big ideas, 6–7
Bureau de Normalisation du Québec
    (BNQ), 38
business, 10, 61
business process modeling notation
    (BPMN), 100

C

Canadian Mental Health Association,
    44, 48
Canadian Public Service, 115
Canadian Standard Association
    (CSA), 38
change management, 107, 110
check-ins, 49, 56, 71, 79
clients
    experience of, 35–36, 63–65
    processes of, 98
    satisfaction of, 35, 43
CMHA National, 44, 49

committees, workplace, 39
communication, 26, 79, 98, 107–8
competency areas, 72, 75
confidentiality, 9
consequences, of doing nothing, 111
Continuous process improvement
    (CPI), 103–4, 110
Covey, Stephen, 6–7
    The Speed of Trust, 6
cycle time (CT), 24

D

Demartini, John, 10
Deming, E., 96, 105, 114
Department of National Defense in
    Canada, 47
development, 40, 53, 70, 72, 74, 86,
    96, 107–8, 112
dimensions, 1–2, 5, 65, 81, 83
Duran, Joseph, 114

E

Employee Assistance Program
    (EAP), 78
employees, 35–36, 107
environment, safe, 5, 38–39, 41, 50,
    63–65, 75, 88
errors, two types of, 66
Everyday Hero Manifesto, The
    (Sharma), 115

www.ingramcontent.com/pod-product-compliance
Lightning Source LLC
Chambersburg PA
CBHW021420210526
45463CB00001B/466